MONEY
& THE HUMAN CONDITION

DOUGLAS OBEY

To Patty & Peter,
All the Best!
Doug

MASON TILER
PUBLISHING

Cover design, interior book design,
and eBook design
by Blue Harvest Creative
www.blueharvestcreative.com

Edited by Linda Sickinger

*Special thanks to my good friend and Author,
Jason Stadtlander for helping me through the nuances
of getting a book published, and to the team of
Blue Harvest Creative for their support and expertise.*

MONEY & THE HUMAN CONDITION

Copyright © 2015 Douglas Obey

All rights reserved. Except as permitted under the U.S. Copyright Act of 1976, no part of this publication may be reproduced, distributed, or transmitted in any form or by any means, or stored in a database or retrieval system, without prior written permission of the publisher.

Published by
Mason Tiler Publishing

ISBN-13: 978-0692486764
ISBN-10: 0692486763

Library of Congress Control Number: 2015911317

Visit the author at:
Website: *www.dougobey.com* & *www.bhcauthors.com*
Facebook: *Douglas-Obey*
Twitter: *@DougObeyAuthor*

Visit the author's website
by scanning the QR code.

TABLE OF CONTENTS

07
INTRODUCTION

11
PART ONE: PHILOSOPHY

13
CHAPTER 1
Capitalism: The Great Equalizer in a Free Society

22
CHAPTER 2
Creating Opportunities

29
CHAPTER 3
Time and Money

35
CHAPTER 4
Financial Planning: Building a Road Map

46
CHAPTER 5
Psychoanalyzing the Economy

65
CHAPTER 6
Stick with Fundamentals

CHAPTER 7
Spirituality: Not at Odds with Capitalism

CHAPTER 8
It's All in Your Mind—So Lose It

CHAPTER 9
Everything's Relative

CHAPTER 10
Priorities and the Fine Art of Balance

CHAPTER 11
Men & Women, Venus & Mars, Security & Living in Tents

CHAPTER 12
Politics: The Good, the Bad and the Ugly

CHAPTER 13
Creativity is Key

CHAPTER 14
The American "Union"

CHAPTER 15
Don't Kill the Golden Goose

CHAPTER 16
The Solution: America's Embrace

PART TWO: THE BASICS

INTRODUCTION

CHAPTER 17
Cash and Bonds

CHAPTER 18
Stocks

CHAPTER 19
Real Estate

CHAPTER 20
Stuff! What Determines Its Value?

CHAPTER 21
Inflation: The Constant Variable

I dedicate this book to my wife Maureen, who has supported me and my every endeavor for over thirty years. There's an old saying that "behind every good man is a better woman" and this couldn't be more true in my case. I couldn't have written this book or had the successful life we've had without her love and encouragement.

INTRODUCTION

THERE MUST BE something wrong! Do you realize you just picked up a book on understanding money and the economy? What's the matter—couldn't you find a good novel?

Or perhaps you are sick of hearing about people no smarter than yourself who are nowhere near as motivated—and *certainly* not as hard-working—getting miles ahead of you financially. Understanding how this can happen is simple really, once you realize how we all interact with money and investments and collectively drive the economy. This is exactly why I have written a book about money and human nature. So if you picked this book up accidentally, consider it fate and keep reading.

We live in a capitalistic society. By its very nature, this means that some will earn more, some less; some will *have* more and some less. Some choose investments that do well. Others don't. Some invest at just the right time while others invest at precisely the *wrong* time. Then again, some don't have the means to invest at all. This is just the way it is.

If you are someone who feels you have simply drawn the short straw, I am going to suggest respectfully that regardless of what has made you feel this way, this book will have you looking at things differently. You might think capitalism doesn't work, but compared to every other alternative—communism, fascism, socialism or a dictatorship—capitalism isn't so bad, and in a free society, it is the best you can hope for by far, *especially* if you want to have any chance at attaining financial independence. If you were lucky enough to have been born into a free, capitalistic society, thank your lucky stars and keep reading to understand why.

So how does money work? What is your perception of money, and is that perception holding you back? Would understanding the dynamics of how you *feel* about money and the perspective others *have* about money assist you in creating solid financial growth opportunities so you no longer rely solely on luck? I am sure you have heard how successful people create their own luck, but what exactly is this success of the so-called "lucky?" And what good is all the money in the world if you can't spend it, or don't have the time to spend it, or don't have anyone to spend it on or with?

Gaining insight and an understanding of these questions is as important as everything else you will learn from reading this book.

First, think of what money *is* and what it *does*. It puts a smile on the face and a tear of happiness in the eye of the bride-to-be when the man she loves presents her with a beautiful diamond. Money fills the refrigerator and gas tank and pays the mortgage or the rent. It provides security and a sense of peace once people are too old to work.

But on the other side of the coin and often to our chagrin, money can buy power and influence politicians. In short, money provides a degree of control as well as the freedom to make choices that enhance our quality of life. But I am reaching beyond the merely materialistic here and talking about *who* and *what* we are as people. I'm referring to what is inherently most important to us all—love, satisfaction, family, comfort, security, power, control and emotional well-being—real stuff, not fluff. I'm talking about the needs and desires of our human nature.

Understanding ourselves and others and what is important to us will help us understand how money, capitalism, emotion and human nature are intertwined. I submit to you that it is important to have a comprehensive knowledge of all four (and much more) to create a truly successful, financially-satisfying life.

As a financial planner with a fascination for economics, I have studied how money works—how it flows from one industry to the next, from one part of the economy to the other, from one country to another. I have learned of the many types of investments designed to take advantage of these flows. I have come to recognize how the government and central banks impact multiple types of investments and the economies of the world. I have identified how a great many dynamic situations affect the flow of money—from politics to social change, government intervention to technology and from increased world trade to environmental issues—and how these, in turn, impact every investment available and the lives of nearly everyone on earth. But most importantly, I deduced quickly that economics is, in fact, a *social* science and as such, deeply rooted in human nature.

Over time, I have come to consider my financial planning practice a microcosm of world economics, learning that counseling people about their finances was based far more on *psychological and emotional* matters than financial investments or money matters. I have also observed that many people possess an adversity to learning about finance—a topic of great importance that profoundly impacts the quality of our lives. You might be surprised to know that I have turned down managing millions of dollars on occasion because the prospective clients refused to try and understand what I was proposing to do with their money. They refused to go through the process of how to accomplish their goals, including the associated risks inherent to any financial product. For good reason, I refused to develop a financial plan for anyone who said, "I do not understand this stuff, and do not want to understand it—I simply want you to take care of it." Abdicating one's financial responsibility is neither a healthy nor a wise choice. As a firm believer in personal responsibility, I determined that turning a blind eye is unacceptable.

I earnestly desire to help you understand money, capitalism, economics and human nature—in a way that you may never have understood it before. And so reading this book will be as much an adventure in understanding the human psyche as it will be in developing discernment in money matters.

That being said, this read will be a study of your emotional *interaction* with money and your practical *response* to the opportunities of living in a free, capitalistic society. For many, the book will be enlightening. For others, it will serve as a compilation of everything previously learned but pieced together in a way that makes perfect sense.

This book is split into two parts. Part One speaks to the human interactive aspects of money and the economy—how self-interest is interwoven and integral to our culture, the motivating force behind the creativity unleashed in a capitalistic society. Part Two focuses on more academic aspects of understanding money and finance, but is written in such a way as to be easily understood—finance "lite" if you will. My goal here is to encourage and persuade you to become part of the process, a process you will come to understand, one that will excite and empower you moving forward.

From these two parts as a whole, the reader will develop a broader knowledge of how money works and how our attitudes about money and finance impact the world around us. The book will "gift" the reader with tools to better attain relative wealth, making for a more content, balanced life. It will also summarize the advantages that a free, capitalistic society provides and suggest potential solutions to make this country even more remarkable than it already is.

Enjoy the ride!

PART ONE
PHILOSOPHY

"I thought I was rich, with a flower that was unique in all the world; and all I had was a common rose."

The Little Prince
Antoine de Saint Exupery

"You shall be free indeed when your days are not without a care nor your nights without a want or a grief, but rather when these things girdle your life and yet you rise above them naked and unbound."

The Prophet
Kahlil Gibran

1
CAPITALISM:
THE GREAT EQUALIZER IN A FREE SOCIETY

OVER THE PAST decade or so, various media factions have vilified capitalism into a four-letter word resulting in many people preferring the term "free markets" instead. However, not only are many markets not as free as they once were, but this terminology only describes one aspect of capitalism. So throughout this book, I use the standard term which I feel is more accurate in an attempt to call it what it truly is—capitalism.

I label capitalism the "great equalizer" for a number of reasons. It's not just because the dynamics of capitalism equalize the supply with the demand. Or that it directs the flow of capital where it may be lacking. Or the myriad of other ways it acts as an equalizer that will be described at greater length throughout this chapter.

Capitalism is an equalizer of societal heritage as well. For many centuries, one's lot in life was dictated by birthright, and seldom did anyone born of one class have the opportunity to break into a higher class. In a free capitalistic society, however, the individual has no bounds other than those self-imposed. You can be born into an extremely poor family yet rise to be fabulously wealthy or acquire a position of tremendous power. This is why capitalism in a free society is the best system possible. It allows the freedom to pursue whatever financial success you are willing to work toward.

Capitalism works because if it is rooted in self-interest. It is in everyone's interest to work hard and benefit accordingly and within the construct of capitalism this can happen. Conversely, in a communist society, it makes little if any difference how hard you work because your standard of living remains the same no matter what you do—and it is human nature for people *not* to work their hardest if there is no reward for doing so.

In truth, with no inherent reward for putting out greater effort, it is in one's own interest to work as *little* as possible. This is why communism is ineffective and can never serve to move individuals forward financially. In practice, it simply works against our human nature, against our self-interest.

Now before I lose you because you simply don't agree with this concept, let me emphasize that self-interest is not always self-ingratiating. It can be very selfless, generous even. For example, if you help an old woman across the street, this is an act of kindness from which you receive a sense of satisfaction. If you get a smile and a "thank you" in return, the good feeling you receive from assisting is your reward for taking a few minutes of your time to help. If you stop to analyze this, you will realize that this good feeling was the very reason you helped in the first place.

Now to prove my point, if the elderly woman rejected your help and struck you with her cane when you took her arm, there would be no reward—no feeling of satisfaction. Consequently, not only would you be reluctant to offer this same woman help in the future, but you would probably think twice about helping any other elderly woman cross the street as well. People will always act in their own interest. Everything we do is motivated by self-interest. Take away the reward, even the intrinsic feel-good reward of this example, and you take away human motivation—and a society with little motivation does not function well, if at all.

You do not have to look to a communist society to see this reward precept in action. You can find it in the projects of cities where many of the people are living on welfare. There, firsthand, you'll typically find the lack of motivation connected to a lack of reward. Many who live in these dependent communities feel—whether true or not—that regardless of personal effort, their situation will not improve. On top of that, they receive a regular check from the government, regardless of what they do or don't do. With these types of disincentives built into the system, it simply does not make financial sense to work hard because the more they work (or the greater their income), the less they receive in ongoing checks from welfare.

There is also little motivation to maintain the property in which they live. If outsiders are responsible for maintenance at no cost to these tenants, why should tenants bother putting in the effort to take care of a place themselves? There is a bit of a slippery slope here in that once people become used to no cause and effect, their dependence on the state grows, and they ultimately lose direct control over their lives. They then derive no personal satisfaction from collecting a check, not having earned it, and this strips them of a level of good feeling and satisfaction—their pride. Without being self-sufficient and in control of their lives, these "feel-good rewards" of gratification and satisfaction slip away, leaving them more vulnerable to other feel-good substitutes such as those found in drugs and alcohol.

This does not have to be the case, however, because in a free, capitalistic society, the means to better oneself exist, and anyone can pursue this path of improvement. I emphasize "free" here because without the freedom to choose and the rights offered the individual in a free society, even capitalism breaks down. This is why I advocate capitalism to be the great equalizer within a free society.

Examples of this are found everywhere and in almost every form. Take the farmer who plants two different crops, tomatoes and lettuce. Let's say that, for whatever reason, there is greater demand for lettuce than tomatoes with the result being too many tomatoes and not enough lettuce. This drives the price of lettuce up as people wanting this limited supply bid higher prices to make sure they get some lettuce. The farmer must now reduce the price of tomatoes as an incentive for people to buy them so they don't rot and go to waste.

Having the freedom to do so, the next time the farmer plants his fields, it is logical to assume that he's going to plant more lettuce and fewer tomatoes. His motivational reward? The higher price of the lettuce and *not* having to lower the price of the tomatoes—giving him more cash in his pocket for the same amount of work in the field. Note that his fields did not get any larger; he simply altered his planting strategy to fit the need.

It is in the farmer's best interest to make as much money as possible for the least amount of effort. The farmer accomplished this by altering his strategy for what he grew. Extrapolating, we humans do this by changing one job for a better one, becoming more efficient (thereby accomplishing the same amount of work in less time), or coming up with new inventions, etc. This is why a free capitalistic society is so dynamic, because within this paradigm, it is in *every* individual's best interest to do more and do better—to become more efficient and to create better systems or gadgets that use less effort, energy, time and material.

Another example of this great equalizer concept is the history of unions in America. The first national union in the United States was formed in 1869. Unions then grew throughout the late 1800s and into the 1900s. The AFL (which stands for the American Federation of Labor, not the football league) was formed in 1904. The reason for this growth was that between the years of 1820 and 1870, and especially during the Industrial Revolution, capitalists like the Vanderbilts and Rockefellers employed millions of workers. Pay was minimal and benefits nonexistent. In addition, working conditions were grueling and in many cases posed potential hazards to the worker. It was in the industrialist's best interest during that time to exploit the masses because he became fabulously wealthy doing so, and this exploitation was possible because jobs were scarce with few work choices available. Hunger is a great motivator regardless of working conditions. This is something most modern-day employees cannot relate to.

But because workers lived in a free society, they were able to organize and make demands of their employer—enter the unions.

As long as employees acted as a unified group and withheld *all* labor until their demands were met, they maintained leverage over the employer. The employer then had to decide if business would remain profitable, (worth his concessions) to meet these demands. If it were still in the employer's best interest to keep the factory open, then the employees were paid higher wages with additional benefits and better working conditions. So unions effectively equalized the exploitation of the employees by increasing wages, adding benefits and bettering working conditions—but they could only do so because a free society allowed this collective bargaining to exist in the first place.

The power that unions wielded served American business notice that if workers were not treated fairly, unions would force them to do so or shut them down. Union membership piqued in the mid-1950s at 35%. But today, according to the 2013 statistics released by the Bureau of Labor Statistics, only around 11.9% of American workers belong to a union. This is a 70-year low, and the majority of those are in public-sector unions (unions that represent our firefighters, police, municipal employees, state workers and many government employees).

Why might union membership be at a 70-year low? In order to retain hard-working loyal workers and to prevent them from organizing, employers added benefits, higher pay and improved working conditions, treating employees much better overall than they had a century or even decades before. Fast forwarding to present day, generally speaking, today's workforce is far too mobile and the demand for good employees too great for employers to mistreat workers. The dire need for unions has therefore diminished. Also, as unions became more powerful and their demands grew, many employers found it no longer profitable to stay in business, either closing up shop or outsourcing their production abroad as a result. In either case, as a consequence, the employees lost jobs and the unions lost members.

Because of capitalism proliferating on a global scale, American unions have lost much of their leverage. Too often, American manufacturing simply found it more profitable to move their production plants abroad, and so the pendulum swung in reverse as unions became a victim of their own success. With unions asking for too much, the great equalizer of capitalism in a free society once again leveled the playing field—but this time on the side of the employer.

Capitalism is the unencumbered flow of supply and demand. As long as people are free to choose where to work, what to buy, where to spend their money and where to invest their savings, then capitalism will be free to iron out the bumps in the dynamic economic environment of supply and demand or the so-called "free markets." Capitalism is so dynamic that it determines how many nurses, engineers, lawyers and teachers are turned out of our colleges and universities every year. For example, when there is a glut of teachers on the market, school systems can get away with offering lower pay due to increased competition for each position. And if teachers are getting paid less, fewer students will choose a teaching degree, resulting in fewer teachers moving out into the workforce and ultimately equalizing the supply with the demand.

Capitalism also determines the number of colleges and universities and what they can charge for tuition. It also keeps standards high, not just in colleges and universities, but everywhere capitalism flourishes. In the case of colleges, if graduates from a particular college are coveted by an industry or workplace in general, that college can charge higher tuition and secure more promising applicants because the demand to go to that college is so great. And if the graduates of that particular college are in greater demand, this warrants higher starting salaries, which in turn justifies higher college tuition.

Capitalism, nationally and worldwide, controls almost everything—from the amount of cars built to the amount of oil pumped, to the price and amount of electricity used and the number of trees cut down and replanted. It also controls which investments perform better than others and is sometimes as simple as how many boxes of cereal are produced in any country within a given year. Capitalism controls the free economies of the world, and the free portions of the not-so-free economies of the world. The capitalistic process is a huge force in all the lives of every human being on this planet and is completely based in human nature. This human "force" which impacts every aspect of life on earth begins with the individual being motivated by his or her self-interest. That force is so powerful that any thing, person, government or policy that runs contrary to the self-interest of the individuals it affects, is doomed to failure.

History is replete with examples of this from the failed or failing welfare policies of the U.S. to the communist government and country of the USSR. It may take time for an ineffective policy to run its course, but such policies will ultimately fail. This is why I consider capitalism and self-interest good, and most things contrary or opposed to self-interest not so good—and in some cases, evil. Capitalism is the means through which self-interest is often expressed.

Our forefathers understood the pursuit of self-interest and that is why they defined the "pursuit of happiness" as one of our inalienable rights in the Declaration of Independence. I also believe that pursuing our self-interest is God's intention for us here on earth, even though this belief is often criticized in discourse around the world. We'll save that one for another day and another chapter.

Please note that when I speak of God, I am not referring to a Christian, Jewish, or Muslim God, Hindu concepts or Buddhist enlightenment. I speak instead in the general sense, of the creator of all entities including human beings. I speak of what I believe to be a universal truth. I speak of a God who set this plan in place and why self-interest is such an integral part of human nature. I speak of God's most precious gift—free will—our unimpeded *right* to choose our own destinies and pursue self-interest.

I will delve further into spirituality and the pursuit of self-interest in a future chapter, but if you think this through, you will more than likely come to an understanding of how it really works and see how the pursuit of happiness (or self-interest) is not actually selfish or bad as some would have you believe.

Often people don't know what will make them happy so they pursue what they *think* will make them happy. Sometimes this happiness quotient is thought to be money and everything money can buy. But once attained, people soon realize the adages of "money can't buy happiness" or "money can't buy love" are true. Money can bring comfort and prestige. It can buy influence and opulence—but it is what you *do* with money and for others that truly brings you happiness. Those "others" may include immediate family or a charity/foundation which develops something to help mankind in general. It needs to be said here that sometimes people waste a lifetime pursuing what they *think* will make them happy only to find it actually doesn't. Unfortunately, that is a road we all travel alone.

Consider some of the happiest moments of your life and they will more than likely be when you helped someone or gave to someone else willingly—not out of guilt or obligation. I'm sure you will agree that when we act out of guilt or obligation, this only builds resentment that does not, in the end, make us happy. It's been my experience that when we give of ourselves freely and willingly, we receive the most fulfillment and enjoyment in return. Sometimes we give more by donating time, opportunity or advice as opposed to monetary gifts. But it is my unwavering belief that only when we have the freedom to pursue self-interest and happiness, only then is there the possibility of achieving tranquility, serenity, peace and true contentment in life.

CAPITALISM: THE GREAT EQUALIZER IN A FREE SOCIETY

There are ideas I will share which are far from new, ideas that I consider to be universal truths. Universal truths are concepts or ideas generally believed to be true, those that are not up for argument or debate—they simply *are*.

I discovered these truths in my own life through various readings and personal life experiences, but I'll strive to share them within the pages of this book in a different light that might offer you a new perspective. One of them is that willingly doing for others brings joy and happiness. Capitalism in a free society releases the splendor of the human spirit, allowing us the freedom and liberty to be all we can be.

2
CREATING OPPORTUNITIES

THE GENERAL BELIEF about opportunities is that they are random, the premise being that an opportunity just sort of shows up without reason, presents itself, and you then determine whether or not to seize it. We hear phrases like "this is the opportunity of a lifetime" implying that this is the only opportunity you will ever have of this magnitude and you'd better jump on it quickly. It is true that some opportunities are indeed both random and exceptional, and therefore opportunities of a lifetime. My experience, however, has been that the majority of opportunities are not as random as they seem. Most, in fact, are not random at all.

We create opportunities all the time or at least set ourselves up to be offered opportunities—even if we do not consciously realize this to be the case. For example, everyone who graduates from high school and *learns* what is taught, sets himself up to acquire employment. With this limited knowledge, he will be valuable to someone by performing a task worthy of payment.

Taking this further, most who graduate from college, having earned a degree, have taken an additional step to become even more valuable by having acquired greater knowledge in a particular field that is needed by an employer. Most think getting a job is simply a natural progression of receiving an education when it is actu-

CREATING OPPORTUNITIES

ally part of the process of creating an opportunity for oneself. When you see opportunities for what they truly are, as a progression of a particular strategy, opportunities abound. More than this, you realize that you are in control of most opportunities arising or being presented to you.

Another way to look at or define opportunities is as solutions to problems. A hospital has a problem when they have patients who need nursing care and not enough nurses to handle the workload. A nursing student graduating from a nursing program has a problem of needing a job that he or she has just spent years learning how to perform. The hospital has the opportunity of employing a well-qualified nurse to help with the workload, and the nursing student has the opportunity to be gainfully employed doing something that is of interest to the student.

Problems solved! Opportunities taken! It may seem strange to look at opportunities in this light, but in order to create opportunities, this is exactly how you have to see them. Wherever a problem exists, therein lies an opportunity.

In the mid '80s, mortgage interest rates began coming down from highs of almost 18%. When these rates started falling, this provided a greater number of people the ability to afford home ownership. Many took advantage of this opportunity—so much so that the demand quickly outstripped the supply of housing and drove the price of real estate to heights never before seen. Within a few short years, houses that in the early '80s might have been selling for $50,000 were easily fetching over $100,000 or more.

This in turn prompted real estate construction of all sorts, flooding the market with a new supply—more supply than the demand could absorb. What looked like a great and fairly safe opportunity while prices were rising, turned into the biggest savings-and-loan crisis this country has ever experienced. Too much supply and not enough demand drove prices down—the first time in generations that real estate prices had fallen. That same cycle duplicated itself over the past decade or so, with prices rising from 2003 through

2007 only to crash in most parts of the country and many parts of the world from 2008 to 2013.

What is that adage? "Those who don't learn from history are destined to repeat it."

In early 1990, the U.S. economy slipped into recession, causing many people to fall behind on mortgage payments and lose their homes to foreclosure. Too many foreclosures caused a number of banks to go under which were then taken over by the federal government. Banks and the FDIC (Federal Deposit Insurance Corporation) then sold the bank-owned real estate in massive auctions across the country. This growing problem then created an opportunity for many people who were capable of buying the auctioned properties for now very low prices. The FDIC and most banks also offered the financing for properties with little money down, making it easier for people to buy them.

I acquired several properties in this way that led to more opportunities in the future. I will offer greater detail and examples of this in Chapter 19 on real estate, but suffice it to say that you did *not* have to be wealthy to take advantage of these opportunities.

I certainly was not. You needed only a willingness to take a risk and nerve enough to withstand the unbridled tension at auctions.

When the FDIC sold off these properties, they did so selling hundreds of properties at once, at about one per minute, in large hotel ballrooms. In order to act quickly, you often had to make nerve-wracking, instant decisions on whether or not to outbid the previous bid from your competition. This frantic pace at auction made it imperative to know and to stick to the maximum price you could afford to bid on the property. But even while striving to maintain this "boundary discipline," it was often tempting to bid just a little higher in hopes of winning. Too much higher, however, could eliminate a property's potential and your ability to make that property work for you. More on how a property works will be explained later in Chapter 19.

CREATING OPPORTUNITIES

Moving forward, after several years of owning a particular building purchased in one of these auctions, another opportunity presented itself. I told a financial-planning client and friend who was interested in diversifying his wealth about these real estate auctions. Up until that point, all his money had been funneled back into his business. However, he did not like the idea of his entire net worth being tied up in his company. So he asked if I would look for an investment property we could buy together to start accumulating assets outside of and unrelated to his business.

As a start, I proposed that he purchase a 50% interest in the building I purchased at auction from the FDIC, and he did. After receiving positive financial reports along with a monthly check for a number of years, my friend wanted more. Realizing the potential there, I proposed another mutual opportunity, one which involved analyzing my personal business and thinking very creatively in order to make this new opportunity come to fruition.

This opportunity was in fact a solution to two problems.

My friend wanted to continue accumulating assets outside of his company but had neither the time nor expertise to do so.

Additionally, he did not particularly care for passive type investments (stocks, bonds, mutual funds, etc.). In my case, like so many other financial planners, I spent half my time working for clients and the other half soliciting new clients. I did not have the time required to look actively for more real estate deals.

So my proposal to my friend was that he fund a real estate venture company with a loan. From those loan proceeds, I would draw a salary equal to half my earnings as a financial planner and spend half my time—the time I would normally spend finding new clients—to instead scope out appealing real estate deals. This way, my existing clients would not suffer, and our venture could get off the ground because I would have the time to run the new business—two problems solved and an opportunity seized to benefit both of us.

The business progressed well as I continued to identify desirable properties, renovate them and sell or retain them as income-producing properties. We remained partners for another four years. During that time, we purchased, renovated and sold many properties—from condos to smaller mansions to log cabins and apartment buildings. One such notable purchase was an old inn and restaurant we razed, building a condominium complex with a total of eleven condos on the site of the old inn. I'll go into these properties in greater detail in another chapter because of the lessons and examples they illustrate.

In our fifth year, my friend and business partner needed additional funds for his growing business. So I bought him out of our business and all mutually-owned properties. To his satisfaction, he had accumulated a tidy sum, one he never would have otherwise acquired, while I ended up owning a lot of properties I never could have accumulated on my own. Out of two problems came a venture opportunity that was not only an overall success, but also a win-win for each of us individually.

I may be stating the merely obvious here, but in order to create opportunities, you have to start with a little creativity and imagination. This requires some thought as to what your natural talents, interests or passions are as well as figuring out how you can benefit from exploiting them. The next logical step is determining exactly how others can benefit as well. This is the beginning of creating a mutually-beneficial financial opportunity.

A little background. I had always possessed an interest in architecture, taking drafting classes in high school and moving on to attain an architectural engineering degree in college. Unfortunately, I graduated into the recessions of the late '70s and early '80s when there was little work for full-blown architects let alone architectural engineers. I did manage to acquire menial jobs in different types of engineering firms for a few years, but after being laid off from my last engineering job, I started selling real estate. I also began investing in real estate and buying what little I could on my own.

CREATING OPPORTUNITIES

Already having a penchant for architecture, it was relatively easy for me to look at a property and visualize what it could be rather than what it was. As a real estate broker, I could then better assess the potential for the property I was selling—whether dealing with the seller in making his property more appealing or working with a buyer in helping him see the potential in a property of interest.

I also did this for myself by renovating the first home I bought and selling it for a substantial profit. I moved on to renovate the second property purchased, a multi-family building, increasing the income I generated from it. A few years after that, I refinanced the property using a 15-year mortgage. This was a step in long-term planning, affording my wife and me the ability to provide a college education for our firstborn son just one year old at the time by either selling or refinancing the property in 15 years when the mortgage would be paid in full and he was nearing college age. As it turned out, this strategy worked incredibly well. Refinancing the property netted not only enough for his college education but also provided us the means to buy more property.

And so it was a natural progression to take on a business partner and create the real estate investment company I spoke of earlier. The business venture was something with which I had both experience and a sound track record. I was subsequently comfortable with replicating this profitable opportunity and could do so without taking an inordinate amount of risk.

There are thousands of stories involving people using creativity to spark thriving multi billion-dollar businesses and achieve wealth well beyond anything I've done. Microsoft, Dell, Amazon, Google, Facebook and Berkshire Hathaway are outstanding examples of this type of success-filled pursuit but are only a few examples of what can be accomplished with a little creativity and a penchant for doing something you are passionate about combined with living in a free, capitalistic society.

Whether the success is enormous as with the companies listed above or relatively small as in my case, the process or formula remains the same. It begins with creating an opportunity around an idea that has the potential to benefit you and others who are willing to go along for the ride. In this country, you're limited only by your imagination and willingness to work hard in shaping that opportunity, *making* it happen, instead of sitting around waiting for happenstance to present itself—the reason so many are eager to immigrate to the U.S. and other free, capitalistic countries. So you see, you should count yourself among the fortunate if you were lucky enough to have been born into a free, capitalistic country like the United States of America.

I'll never forget the night I was waiting tables in my late twenties and serving two businessmen. For much of the evening, they were speaking to each other in German. After paying their bill, I thanked them for their generous tip. The older of the two then asked me if I wanted a far more valuable tip. Not really understanding the meaning behind his question, he followed with a phrase spoken in German. Still not understanding, I asked him what it meant in English.

His response? "In America, there is gold in the streets. All you have to do is bend over and pick it up." He was clearly referring to the incredible opportunities available in our country. This was true then, and is still true now.

3

TIME AND MONEY

THE PRIOR CHAPTER illustrates an opportunity and partnership arising from a solution to the challenge of one person having money but no time and the other having time and expertise but lacking money. This example exemplifies what is fundamental to all good investments.

Time and money are not only fundamental to a good investment but are also important in our lives. Most people have either one or the other but seldom both. As a matter of fact, unless you're independently wealthy or living off a trust fund, you usually have one problem or the other. This is actually a case in point for capitalism being a great equalizer.

For those working far too many hours per week, the net cost of living is much higher simply because they don't have the time to shop for bargains. The market depends on this because it couldn't offer the deep discounts and sales on items if not selling enough merchandise at full price.

Conversely, if not working long hours, in all likelihood, you aren't making much money, but because you pay less income tax and can shop for bargains, your lifestyle isn't as dissimilar from your higher-earning neighbor as the variance in your incomes might suggest.

Many of us have been in both places but at different times in our lives. When you are young and starting out, your salary is often lower, but you have the time to rummage through the clothing racks for discounted clothing until you find high-quality clothes at bargain prices—the net result being that you look as well-dressed as someone affording full price.

As we get older, however, with higher salaries and greater responsibilities, we don't have the time to shop for the bargains but can afford more expensive clothing, paying higher prices for the same well-dressed look. Upscale clothing stores depend on selling enough at higher prices so when they have to clear the racks for next season's styles and sell the remaining clothing to the discounters, they still make a profit overall.

To put this in proper perspective, consider this example. Let's take a men's suit selling for $1,500 in an upscale clothing store. In order to buy that $1,500 suit, after paying state and federal taxes, the consumer has to earn upwards of $2,500. On the other hand, six months later, that same suit at a discount store might cost only $400—and after taxes, the person buying this suit might only have to earn $500. That's less than a quarter of the amount the full-price buyer has to earn for the same item. One buyer spends his time to save money, and the other buyer spends his money to save time.

Taking advantage of this time/money concept is where many opportunities arise. If you have time but little money, you can offer a service to someone who has little time but more money. This solves a problem for each individual, rendering it a win-win. This is because the less you have of something, the more you value it—and it is this difference in perceived value that is an integral part of our capitalistic system. A person with little money would never pay someone to rake his yard if capable of doing it himself because the money it would cost is more valuable to him than the time it would take. Conversely, someone with a lot of money would probably value the time saved more than the money it would cost to have someone else do it.

TIME AND MONEY

All investing takes time and money. If you put a dollar down on the color red at the roulette table and win, you double your money, and it took no time. That is why this is called gambling and not investing. Investing in anything worthwhile requires a heavy dose of due diligence as well as a parcel of time in order for that investment to accomplish its intended purpose.

In the case of stocks, we often hear that the way to make money is to "buy and hold." The theory is that if you did your homework enough to determine a company to be a worthwhile investment, enough to buy its stock, then the company should remain solid with the same prospects for growth years or decades later. Chances are, therefore, that time will reveal the potential you saw in it when you made the purchase—unless the fundamentals of the company change significantly during that period. To buy a stock only to sell it three or six months later is the equivalent of gambling here. We've all heard "patience is a virtue," and it's especially virtuous and often profitable in the stock market—providing you've done your homework.

While I'm on the topic of stock-market homework, I would guesstimate that 99.99% of people who invest in individual stocks can't do the necessary homework because they simply don't know how to analyze a company. Consequently, they rely on information from analysts, investment newsletters, stock brokers and a myriad of other sources. It is important to note that the more removed the source is from you, the more objective that source may be—as in the case of an investment newsletter.

On the other hand, if someone such as a Wall Street analyst or stock broker makes money directly from your purchase and recommends an investment in a particular stock, their objectivity should come into question immediately. This is why I seldom recommend investing directly in individual stocks unless the person advising you is trustworthy and has a successful investment track record proving him savvy enough to complete his own thorough analysis.

The best way for the average person to invest in the stock market is through mutual funds, ETFs (exchange-traded funds) and/or managed accounts. Not only does a fund diversify your investment, lowering the risk, but it also provides an avenue for investing in a greater number of stocks than you could typically afford on your own.

In addition, the fund's manager, the individual or group of individuals who make the decisions on buying and selling, have an interest aligned with the investor. In most cases, the fund manager's livelihood *depends* on how well he manages the fund. If he does a good job, he makes big bonuses, often many times larger than his base salary. On the other hand, if he performs badly, he could be out of a job. This is the kind of consequential pressure I want the person or persons in charge of making fund decisions to have—an interest aligned directly with yours as the investor.

It needs to be said, however, that there is still due diligence required on your part when purchasing a mutual fund, ETF or managed account. It is important for you to determine how the fund has performed versus its peers over time—preferably a good five or 10-year track record.

I say "versus its peers" rather than versus the market for the following reason. Let's say you choose to invest in a category that has been out of favor for the past five years and maybe even lost money. You can still select a good mutual fund in that category by comparing which one lost *less*. The next step is to make sure the person or team that produced this track record is still there managing the fund. Often mutual-fund companies will take managers who have shown themselves to be successful with smaller funds and move them into larger funds, placing a new manager who was not responsible for that fund's track record in charge of the smaller fund. In that case, you'd be investing in a fund with a great track record but currently being run by an individual who may not have the knowledge and expertise to replicate that track record in the future.

The last thing I'll mention about mutual funds, ETFs and managed accounts is that, even though the majority of funds do not match the average return of the index they compare to, I still prefer managed funds to index funds. We've all heard the adage "buy low and sell high." Without getting too complicated here, index funds by their very nature do just the opposite and tend to perform well only in up markets. If you are buying and holding for a significant time frame, then you will experience up and down markets, and it's better to have an experienced person pulling the strings behind your fund as opposed to a computer program. Also, if you like the concept of index funds, I would suggest you look into something called fundamental index funds. These funds value stocks in an index on more of a fundamental basis rather than only market price and proportion the stocks in the fund accordingly. This makes them part of a more *value-oriented* investment philosophy.

Real estate investments take not only time and money but often require leverage. Borrowing a portion of the purchase price can play a large part in a real estate investment, making it riskier than people perceive them to be.

Let me explain what I mean here. Let's say you buy an investment property for $1,000,000 that is earning, after all expenses, $60,000. If you paid cash for the property, that would amount to a 6% cash-on-cash rate of return. Let's say then that in a given year a quarter of the building went unrented for whatever reason and resulted in earnings of only $45,000 that year—your rate of return would have simply fallen by 1.5%, from 6% to 4.5%. Now let's say that in that same year prices for real estate softened by 20%. Then your equity would have fallen by $200,000 or 20%, and your investment is only worth $800,000. With me so far?

Now let's add leverage or a mortgage to the purchase. Most banks look for at least 25% down from the buyer of investment properties, so we'll assume a 75% mortgage or $750,000 on the $1,000,000 price of the building. Assuming a 5% interest rate on the note and a 25-year amortization (payback schedule), the payment would be $4,385 per month or $52,620 per year—leaving you with a $7,380 cash-on-cash return on your $250,000 investment that equates to about an 3% return. This doesn't include the principal that is being paid down on the mortgage note each month.

Taking the same circumstances into consideration as in the previous scenario, if for whatever reason, one quarter of the building went unrented in any given year, you are losing money and have a negative return on your investment. Instead of your rate of return simply falling from 6% to 4.5%, it falls from a positive 3% to a negative 3%, and if you can't come up with the difference each month from other sources, you are now falling behind in the mortgage or other expenses on the building. Now let's add in the value dropping by 20%. Instead of simply losing $200,000 (or 20% of your equity) you now lose $200,000, but it represents 80% of *your* equity of $250,000.

Leverage adds significant risk to any investment whether you're mortgaging real estate or buying stock on margin, but it allows you to buy more than you could otherwise afford. This is great when real estate prices are climbing but can get ugly during a downturn. Leverage therefore equals more of an opportunity but with greater risk.

4

FINANCIAL PLANNING: BUILDING A ROAD MAP

MANY PEOPLE THINK financial planning is paramount to rocket science, requiring an understanding of everything from economic statistics to corporate financial reports. The truth is that even those who might understand such things don't necessarily accomplish putting together an appropriate financial plan—nor do they always understand how to make money work for them as opposed to working for their money.

Putting together an effective financial plan has more to do with common sense, human nature and feelings about risk than it does financial analysis. What it really takes and what most people don't do, is putting time and careful thought into the process. Most people simply think making some good investments will do. While this is good, it is not enough nor is it the most important part of a sound financial plan.

First you have to establish your objectives. What exactly are you trying to accomplish? Why go through this exercise to begin with? There needs to be an overriding reason guiding your efforts here. That reason could be buying a home, providing a college education for your children, investing for retirement or attaining financial independence. It could be as simple as living a comfortable lifestyle with few other long-term goals. Whatever your reason is, it must be quantified in order for you to know what you are trying to accomplish and guide the process toward that end.

Let's use the example of a young couple with the objective of buying their first home. Since most people don't pay cash for a house, the first question to ask themselves is, "How much money can we afford each month toward the payment of a mortgage used to purchase a home?" The second question is, "What does a house in the desired geographic area with the amenities we want cost?" To answer these questions, they would have to determine how much money they bring home every month and the total of their current monthly expenses.

Let's say they determine they have a combined after-tax monthly income of $7,000. Next, they have to decide how comfortable they are using both incomes in calculating what they would have available for a house payment. Note that non-monetary preferences and their risk tolerance as a couple would play a part in these answers. If the couple intends to have children, with one parent staying home as caregiver, then it is essential to use only the working spouse's income when determining what they could afford in a mortgage payment.

Or maybe they do not want children but are uncomfortable planning on a payment requiring both to be working at all times. They simply wish to avoid the affordability issue if one were to be laid off or lose a job for any reason. Taking into account their risk tolerance in such a case may reduce the amount of money they are willing to commit to a monthly mortgage payment.

For example, let's assume they are comfortable with counting on a $4,000 after-tax monthly income with their current expenses (excluding rent or housing costs) at $1,500. In this case, they would have $2,500 left to commit to a home payment. However, that amount should include not only the principal and interest for the mortgage payment but also real estate taxes and homeowners' insurance.

The next step would be sitting down with a real estate agent, mortgage broker or banker to determine how much of a mortgage and home payment $2,500 per month would afford based on current interest rates and the length of time you would like the term of the mortgage to be. For the purpose of this example, assume the result was that they could afford a $300,000 loan. To avoid mortgage insurance, a 20% down payment would be required ($75,000) along with approximately $5,000 in closing costs.

Now, after completing this groundwork, they know the exact amount of money to save in order to accomplish their goal of buying a home—provided a home with the amenities they wanted and in a location they were comfortable with existed in their price range. At this point, they need to sit down with a real estate agent and look at some homes that fit their criteria to determine what those homes are selling for. If a home matching these criteria exists, then the process becomes as simple as figuring out how much they can put away each month and how many months it would take to save a total of $80,000.

This is the basic process required for each financial objective you have. The complexity of quantifying objectives is the biggest reason many people don't bother planning, but without a planning road map, it is difficult to arrive at the desired destination. Helping people with this process is how the financial planning industry came into being.

After establishing goals and quantifying objectives, you need to determine your risk tolerance, and not just from an investment point of view but from a "life" perspective. Thinking it through, what will happen if one of you dies—can you or your spouse live on the remaining income? How much will your surviving spouse need if you were to pass on? And what would happen if one income "dies" because of a disability?

These considerations are easily calculated but need serious thought. Unexpected events can and do occur, and the resulting loss of income needed to cover your living expenses is one of the primary causes in home foreclosures. The good investment you spent hours researching will not last long in the event of a death or long-term disability. It is therefore imperative to make sure these two risks are properly covered. Most other types of insurance such as home and auto are required. Life and disability insurance are not required but *should* be as they are most important in maintaining your current lifestyle and providing financial security.

Once this income-security issue is taken into consideration, then you can think about investing. Consider the following. What is your investment risk tolerance? Do high-risk or volatile investments keep you from sleeping at night? And what is your estimated time horizon—when are you going to need the money from your investment? It is important to determine your comfort level. No investment, regardless of its potential, is worth adding a heavy burden in worry and stress.

So to sum it up, if the investment has a high potential for loss, you should only invest money you can afford to lose. Makes sense, right? Don't allow greed to override your comfort level. Typically, high-risk investments have the potential for high reward, but regardless of how much money you *might* make, the investment is not worth it if you are fearful, playing with money you can ill afford to lose, and that fear is keeping you up at night. If you invest under these circumstances, it's almost inevitable that you will lose money because your own human nature will be working against you.

Let me illustrate. Assume you invested money you really couldn't afford to lose in a potentially high-flying stock. Say you bought the stock at $20 per share and purchased enough shares so that the total investment was an amount that was very meaningful to you, relatively speaking.

Moving forward, the stock goes up to $24 after the first month. Would you sell? Unlikely, as the stock is doing what you expected. After the second month, it's valued at $27. Would you sell? Ditto. Then after the third month, it's dropped to $22. Would you sell? Again unlikely, when you could have sold for a much higher price only one month earlier.

Another month goes by and your stock drops to $17. Would you sell? What—and take a loss?! The next month it goes back up to $20. Would you sell? Not likely. Why now when it's back on track and you haven't made anything anyway? Next month it's up to $26. Would you sell? No—not while it's taking off.

The following month it's up to $30. Would you sell? Ditto. The month after that it drops to $24. Would you sell? Maybe the next time it hits $30. A month passes and it drops to $18. Would you sell? Nope. You're only losing a few bucks per share and its value has bounced around anyway, so you'll wait until it bounces higher. But the next month it drops to $13. Would you sell? The loss hurts, but it's *only* on paper...unless you sell, and then it's real.

Next month it drops to $10. Would you sell? Ouch. That hurts, especially with the investment being money you can't afford to lose. But you've already lost this much, it's unlikely to drop much further and at this point you simply want to break even before you get out.

The next month it drops to $7. Would you get out? Panic is setting in, but you really hate locking in such a huge loss if you don't have to. Another month passes and its value drops again—to $5. Would you sell? Very likely, especially because the damn thing just seems to be dropping further and further and you don't want to lose everything. Remember this is money you can't afford to lose.

This progression of thought and emotion will occur every time you put money into a high-risk investment in an attempt to make a killing with money you can't afford to lose. Greed will keep you from selling if the investment goes up because you'll be feeling good, very smart, and you're "playing with the casino's money." It's only when it drops below your threshold of pain—and we all have it—that fear forces you to sell and realize the loss.

A case in point is the Fidelity Magellan Fund, one of the most successful funds of the 1980s and early 1990s. Fidelity completed a study and found that the average investor in the fund actually lost money even though the fund did extremely well over those years. The reason is that people typically buy after the fund has a great run-up, wanting to participate in the gains (buying high), but when the fund went down, people sold (selling low). Had they simply stayed in, they would have done well over the years—but human nature is such that it's nearly impossible to do this with money you can ill afford to lose.

Financial planning has basic common-sense rules to follow. The first is to insure against losses you can't afford to incur. As we've already covered, most types of insurance are required—home and car insurance, for example. Others like life, disability and liability (because of our ever-increasing litigious society) need to be addressed as well.

Next you need to establish an emergency fund—money set aside in the event there is an unexpected expense or loss of income, in order to keep things going. This is something they don't write insurance for, like losing your job or your furnace dying. Depending on your risk tolerance, you can create an emergency fund by either saving money in an ultra-safe investment vehicle—like a savings account, CD or money market account, or if you own a home, by securing a home equity line of credit.

I say "depending on your risk tolerance" because many ultra-conservative people would have a hard time going into debt in the event of a job loss or major unplanned expense. For these people, an emergency fund of at least three months' living expenses is necessary with six months' expenses being preferable. This money should only be invested in ultra-conservative *liquid* investments which means the money is sure to be there and available at any point in time with no possibility of loss. By their very nature, these are considered "lazy" dollars which means they don't typically work hard to earn income, delivering little return. But understand that the purpose here is for those funds to be available at a moment's notice in the event of an emergency.

As an aside, don't make the mistake of letting your stock portfolio substitute for an emergency fund. Stocks are marketable, not liquid. In other words, stocks must be sold prior to accessing your money and can be sold only if there is someone who will buy. Typically, selling is not a problem—*but at what price*? The amount of money you funded the portfolio with may not be there when you need it because stocks can go down as well as up.

For those with high enough risk tolerance and the fiscal discipline to use the money only for emergencies, an equity line of credit can double as an emergency fund but must be established before you actually need to draw from it. It's unlikely that a bank or other lending institution is going to approve you for any additional loan or line of credit in the event you've lost your job and can't show how this debt will be repaid. An equity line should be as substantial as possible. The advantage here is that the funds will be available at a moment's notice as long as they have not been used for non-emergency items like new furniture or a vacation. This allows you the ability to invest what you would normally put in an emergency fund into harder-working (albeit riskier) investments but still have the funds set aside to draw from via the home equity line in the event of an emergency. The other advantage of the home equity line? There is no cost or interest to pay unless you use the money. Obviously, this option requires owning a house with enough equity to acquire an appropriate line of credit.

The next rule is to never let the tax tail wag the dog. What I mean by this is that the tax consequences from any investment, good or bad, should never be the determining factor for investing in or maintaining an investment. Let me give an example. Let's say you've owned an investment for six months. It has done well but for whatever reason, you feel it is more likely to lose value from this point on rather than continuing to go up or even maintain its value. If you sell, you will pay short-term capital gains tax on the profit made—not having held it for at least a year which is required to qualify for long-term capital gains tax treatment.

Let's assume you are in the 28% federal income tax bracket. By selling after six months, the gain would be subject to your income tax bracket rate of 28%. If you hold it for at least one year, the gain will qualify for the long-term capital gains rate of 15%. Because your out-of-pocket tax rate is about half here, the temptation is to hold off selling the investment, waiting the additional six months to avoid paying Uncle Sam more than you absolutely have to.

Waiting this additional six months is an excellent example of letting the tax tail (or the tax benefits associated with the decision) wag the dog. The dog—the bigger, more important part of the decision—is what you would do if tax rates were not a consideration. Many people in this situation, trying to avoid the higher tax rate, have watched their gain disappear during the time they've held out waiting to pay a lower tax and thereby paid the ultimate 100% tax because they forfeited the gain altogether.

So always remember that half a loaf is better than no loaf at all. Taxes are only due if you make money. Making money is beneficial even if a portion of what you make is reluctantly paid to the IRS because you get to keep the difference. In the case above, if the gain evaporated over the six months, it's true you would have beaten the IRS out of money—*but only by not making any*. This is crazy and a classic example of letting the tax tail wag the dog.

That being said, effective financial planning must take into account the tax implications of any actions you take. For example, say you owned an investment property held for quite a while which had substantially depreciated for tax purposes. Just to clarify, when you own an investment property, the tax code allows/forces you to take a depreciation deduction each year.

That deduction is typically based on a 27.5 year lifespan of the property set by the tax code. So you can take a deduction for 1/27.5 or 3.64% of the value of the building (but not the land) each year. Let's use an example of a piece of investment property that you purchased for $500,000 in which the land was worth $100,000. Each year, along with other normal expenses, you would take a deduction for 3.64% of $400,000 (the value of the building alone) or $14,560. This is one of the tax benefits to owning investment property. When you sell the property, however, you must "recapture" the depreciation at a 25% tax rate.

Going back to the $500,000 investment property, if you owned it for 27 ½ years, you would have completely depreciated it. So from a capital-gains-tax point of view, the basis in the property would simply be the $100,000 value of the land itself. If you then sold the property, you would pay capital gains tax on the *difference* between the selling price and the $100,000 basis in the property. Even though you paid $500,000 for the property, because you depreciated it and took a tax deduction each year for that depreciation, you have in essence told the IRS that over the past 27 ½ years, the property (other than the land) has no value. So when you sell it for more than the land value of $100,000, likely the case, you have to declare the amount above the $100,000 basis as a capital gain.

If you were to sell that investment property for $1,000,000, twice what you paid for it 27 ½ years ago, you would deduct the basis or $100,000 from the sale price of $1,000,000 and claim $500,000 of the $900,000 as a long-term capital gain currently subject to a 15% or 20% tax rate, and $400,000 of recaptured depreciation at a 25% rate. The total, assuming a 20% capital gain rate, would be a whopping $200,000 that you would owe in federal tax. If applicable, additional state tax might apply as well.

If all this isn't complicated enough, here's where additional financial analysis comes in. If you sold the investment property and used the proceeds to reinvest in something else, that something else would have to work even harder than the property does for you because you are starting with less money to begin with—because of the tax haircut taken when you sold the property.

Returning to our example, let's assume the $1,000,000 property was netting you a return of 7% or $70,000 each year. If you sell the property for $1,000,000 and pay federal taxes of $200,000, you would only have $800,000 left to invest. This amount would actually be even less because you would incur selling expenses like real estate commissions, closing costs and possibly even state capital gains taxes. But keeping it simple, you would have $800,000 in proceeds from the sale. In order for this amount of money to give you the same $70,000 return, you would need an 8.75% rate of return where the $1,000,000 property was only earning a return rate of 7% (as noted above).

The tax consequences of investments must be considered when buying or selling but should never be the sole basis for your decision, merely a part of it. In this example, where the proceeds were simply reinvested, if the investment considered were not yielding 8.75% to match what the real estate was yielding, then the owner may consider not selling and hanging on to the building. Typically, however, there are other overriding reasons for the sale of a property or investment, and those reasons should always take precedence. Never let the tax tail wag the dog.

Another tax consideration when investing is whether to purchase tax-free, tax-deferred or taxable investments. You can buy certain bonds to garner a tax-free or partially tax-free return on your money, but to determine whether this makes sense, you must analyze what the after-tax return would be on both. All other factors being equal, go with the higher after-tax return whether in a tax-free or taxable bond.

If the money being invested is intended for retirement, you can wrap an otherwise taxable investment in an IRA or other tax-deferred retirement vehicle, and as long as you abide by the rules governing that vehicle, defer the tax until you actually take the money out of the IRA, 401k or other retirement account. Another option is to wrap an otherwise taxable investment in a Roth IRA where, as long as you abide by the rules of the Roth IRA, you avoid any income or capital gains tax on the earnings altogether. To determine which "wrapper" to use for retirement assets, look at your current tax bracket as well as the bracket you expect to be in when you retire. Admittedly, making this determination can be challenging, especially if you have many years before retirement, but you can seek financial guidance in doing so.

FINANCIAL PLANNING: BUILDING A ROAD MAP

If the investment is designed to pay for future college expenses, there are still other tax-deferred wrappers the government allows to make saving for college a little easier. But suffice it to say, if you are planning for specific future financial needs such as this, you need to know what options are available and proceed in the most tax-efficient manner.

With the myriad of tax-qualified plans and thousands of investments available, the most important rule to building wealth, relatively speaking, is a simple one: LIVE BENEATH YOUR MEANS and save or invest the difference.

Following this rule doesn't guarantee a financially independent future, but is your best shot at attaining one. Beyond this, a sound financial plan or road map is all you need to get you where you want to go.

5

PSYCHOANALYZING THE ECONOMY

ECONOMICS ISN'T ROCKET science. Actually, it's far more difficult to understand. Rocket science is based in fact, logic, mathematical reason and applying the laws of physics. If you learn and understand the concepts involved and know the theorems, you can figure it out, especially with the computer applications available today. You can then apply that knowledge to launch rockets, set satellites into orbit and utilize lots of other cool applications that make life better for mankind.

Economics, on the other hand, is a whole other can of worms. Completely understanding our economy (or the economies of the world now that we are entrenched in a global economy) is virtually impossible. The conceptual understanding itself isn't impossible. It's identifying all the aspects and variables and then properly gauging and measuring them that is nearly impossible. This is because the economy, with its many technicalities, is still ultimately anchored in human nature. And while human nature can be predicted to some degree, it maintains an element of irrationality innate to all human beings.

Humans are emotional beings and emotions aren't always logical or predictable. Case in point. A woman loses her job. Knowing how depressed she is, her husband returns home with flowers. Instead of receiving the desired gratitude response from his wife of, "Aww, honey, they're beautiful! Thanks for being so thoughtful," he gets the angry response of, "I've had a frustrating day looking for a job and wondering how we are going to pay the mortgage—and you are out wasting money on stupid *flowers* that will only die? What are you thinking? Obviously, you *aren't* thinking. But then, what's new about *that*?" I think this ever-present element of human nature is the reason the vast majority of economists are wrong in prognosticating both the markets and the future of the economy. Emotions play a part in decision-making, affecting our monetary choices, and are difficult if not impossible to predict.

That being said, how does the average person like yourself figure it all out? The simple answer is you can't, but you *can* understand what moves the markets that drive the economy. Being human and dealing directly with an economy based in human nature, you can become an astute observer and psychoanalyze how you and others are feeling about financial markets and the economy. You can then use your microcosm, you and the people you know, to make assumptions about the overall macrocosm—the economy as a whole.

Here's an example. Your company has just announced it will be experiencing lay-offs in the next quarter. Your next-door neighbor's wife has lost her job and is having a difficult time finding another. Next you note that the popular restaurant where you always have to wait for a table isn't busy lately. Given this limited scenario of economic change, it is reasonable to assume that you and people in general will be more cautious with discretionary spending.

Listening to a bit of economic news can verify whether your scenario is an isolated case or becoming the norm. If it is being reported that this scenario is prevalent nationwide, then it is also reasonable to assume that retailers, especially those selling discretionary items, will be selling less merchandise and therefore making lower profits.

The next step would be to assume those retailers will probably be laying off workers. As a result, those laid-off employees won't be spending as much money, further adding to a slowing economy. You could also go out on a limb and assume that the businesses which aren't impacted as much as retailers, believing the economy is slowing down, might be more cautious in hiring new employees. You could go on and on with similar assumptions, probably leading to the same conclusion—that the economy is indeed beginning to slow. You get an "A!" Now what do you do with your astute conclusion?

A logical reaction might be to call your 401k custodian and request an exchange of the money invested in that stock fund that hasn't been doing much of anything lately and consider putting it into something a little safer, like a bond fund or money market fund. This way, as the economy softens and companies sell less stuff (making lower profits, a key component of a stock's price) and the stock market begins dropping, you won't lose any money in your 401k—that is, if you are correct and that stock fund in your 401k follows the market, dropping in value.

But what if you are wrong? Or worse yet, what if you are right and the stock market falls but that stock fund in your 401k bucks the trend and actually goes up? What then? Not probable, but certainly possible. Most likely, because of human nature, you would feel you made a mistake and justify getting back into the fund, convincing yourself that your logic must be faulty and you are not smart enough to figure this stuff out. Then after getting back in, your fund starts following the market down, but you are afraid to get out again because of what happened when you did before—so you stay in and watch the value drop further and further, eroding your much-needed retirement savings.

There are several lessons I'd like to point out here because this is where many find themselves today, feeling they are not smart enough to figure this stuff out but also having been brainwashed to "buy and hold," that it's "not timing the market but time in the market" that will be profitable. Depending on what time period you are talking about, this isn't necessarily true.

What's true is that buying and holding will get you close to the same return that the market yields over the period of time that you buy and hold—assuming you are investing in funds or indexes that are broadly invested. If you are investing in individual stocks, then anything goes because individual stocks can more easily buck the trend, dropping in an "up" market or rising in a "down" market. Unless you have specific, credible information about a particular stock you are investing in, it is pretty much a crap shoot. Buying and holding, whether in a broad-based fund or individual stocks, is by no means a formula for successful investing, depending on the fundamentals of the time period you are investing in.

Here are several examples of times when buying and holding proved less than profitable. In October of 1961, if you bought the S&P 500 stock index (the equivalent of buying stock in the 500 largest companies in the U.S. and a broad measure for the market as a whole) and sold 13 years later, you would have lost over 11% of your money and would have taken 13 years to do so. Or if you bought in the fall of 1972 and sold 10 years later, you wouldn't have made a dime but simply wasted 10 investment years. More currently, if you invested in the S&P 500 in the fall of 1999 and got out in the panic of late 2008 and early 2009, you would have lost money and have wasted almost 10 years doing so. But investing at these "wrong" times would have been a very compelling move because prior to the fall of 1999, the market had its best run *ever* in the history of the stock market. During the eight years prior to the fall of 1961, the market almost tripled in value, making that "wrong time" a seemingly compelling time to invest as well.

There are many other examples, but with clarity and hindsight, the obvious conclusion is that bear (down) markets follow bull (up) markets and vice versa. However, history also shows that bear markets have a somewhat shorter duration than the bull markets they follow.

So let's go back a few paragraphs. After verifying the scenario in your microcosm was similar to what is happening nationally, your logical conclusion to get out of the stock fund in your 401k plan and move into something safer is confirmed. Your decision is based logically on the fundamentals of the current economy. The analysis of fundamentals, if accurate, always wins out. It is very difficult, if not impossible, for a company's stock to rise if that company's profits are dropping—not impossible, because rumor and emotion can rule the day—but typically, over an extended period of time, fundamentals win out. You should therefore stick with your decision to get out of the stock fund in your 401k.

How else can we benefit from analyzing the economy? And what other conclusions can we readily make without needing to be a rocket scientist? How about the type of mortgage to take out? It only makes sense that if you are expecting interest rates to rise, you would avoid adjustable rate mortgages (ARMs) as they tend to follow interest rates, taking instead a fixed mortgage which locks in the rate even though this fixed-rate mortgage typically starts at a higher rate than an ARM. And it stands to reason that the reverse is also true. If you expect interest rates to drop in the future, you might not want to lock in today's higher rates with a fixed-rate mortgage but instead, opt for an ARM.

The challenge here is figuring out which direction interest rates are likely to go. This is actually even more difficult than trying to predict the direction of the stock market. Your first question might be to ask yourself who or what controls interest rates. The short answer—and we are definitely trying to keep it short—is that the Federal Reserve determines short-term rates by setting what they call the "discount rate." This is the rate at which banks can borrow from the Federal Reserve, if necessary. Banks then typically set their prime rates at 3% above this Federal Reserve discount rate. Currently, the discount rate is at .25% and prime rate is 3.25%.

Even though banks don't typically borrow from the Federal Reserve, they still use this discount rate as a benchmark for a myriad of banking products—from CDs to checking and savings accounts. These banking instruments are where banks get their money to do business in the first place, from you and me, their depositors. You and I deposit our money into a CD paying, say 1%, and the bank uses that money to give someone else a loan, at say 5%. The difference between what the bank pays you on the CD and the rate they charge on the loan is their cash flow. What remains after their expenses is their profit. Of course, they can't loan out everything they take in because they need to service customers who make withdrawals from their bank accounts. This is where the Federal Reserve comes in again, by establishing how much money banks must keep on hand from their deposits in reserve.

Okay. Enough about banking. We're trying to figure out how to predict the direction of interest rates.

To some degree, however, what banks are paying and charging, coupled with what's going on in the economy, has a lot to do with getting clues about where rates may be headed. Unfortunately, when most people are saving money, they don't give much thought to the most important aspect of their savings—the purchasing power of those savings. It's a rather difficult concept to grasp because we tend to value the actual dollars rather than what those dollars can buy. We all know that dollar bills have no real value in and of themselves except for the scrap of paper they are printed on, but we seldom think of currency in this way because it can be readily traded for goods or services. It's the value *assigned* to dollars (based on the goods they can be traded for) that establishes their true value.

The fact that we honor this value is what makes currency work in the first place. It's only this purchasing power that has any real clout, and this is determined every day through wholesale and retail outlets as well as service providers across the nation. Some days, for instance, a store may value its merchandise dearly, setting higher prices. But following a few days of the store not selling their merchandise at these higher prices, they will realize that the public disagrees with the value placed on that merchandise—and will drop their prices in order to continue selling. Similarly, some days a kid, not needing the money as much, will charge $25 to mow your lawn. On other days, however, needing the money right now for something in particular, he might mow your lawn for only $15.

This leads to what we've always heard is the cornerstone of economics—supply and demand. If we simply use the laws of supply and demand in our banking scenario, it might look something like this. A bank is in the business of buying and selling money. Let's say they put out a sign stating they will pay 1% for deposits, but thinking this percentage is not high enough, people don't deposit any money. If the bank has no deposits, they can't make loans (assuming the complicated Federal Reserve banking system didn't exist). And if they don't make any money, they will soon go out of business. So they increase the rate to 2%, and people start depositing their money.

Okay, so the bank has solved one end of the transaction. Now that they have money in their vaults, they put out a sign offering loans at a rate of 6%. Unfortunately, no one is interested in paying this high of a rate resulting in nobody requesting a loan. Without being able to earn interest on the money in their vault, they will not make any money to pay the depositors, eventually going out of business.

So they drop their loan rate to 5% and people begin taking out loans. Now they have interest dollars coming in to pay the interest owed to their depositors as well as some extra to pay the tellers, heating bills, rent and other expenses. Demand determined what the bank paid for deposits which in turn determined the supply of dollars the bank had to loan out. The demand for loans also determined what banks could charge for loans.

Now let's add inflation to the mix. How much more "stuff" will cost in the future should be important to someone making deposits in a bank and determine to a degree what interest rate they are seeking as a rate of return on their money. Logic will tell you that people making deposits will desire the ability to purchase more with that money once they get it back from the bank.

So let's assume that prices in general are going up by 4% per year. Knowing that the interest earned is considered income (and therefore taxable), we first have to figure out the tax rate we would have to pay and what we would be left with after. If our tax rate is 20%, we will need to earn at least 5% from the bank just to stay even. The math looks like this. Let's say $100 is deposited and earns 5% or $5 over the course of a year. The taxing authorities (state and federal) tax that $5 at a 20% rate which equals $1. So after tax, the depositor is left with $104, and if inflation is running at 4%, then what cost $100 last year when the deposit was made, now costs $104—and the depositor has gained nothing in the way of purchasing power. Taking this into account, it is logical that the depositor would demand a higher rate than 5% paid on his deposits in order to be better off a year later for allowing the bank to use his money during that time.

If the bank needs to make a 3% spread on deposits (the difference between what it pays and what it charges), then it would have to charge 9% for loans so that after it takes the 3% spread needed to stay in business and make a profit, it could pay the depositor 6%—so the depositor would get what is called a "real" rate of return on his deposit (in this case, almost 1%). The real rate of return is the increase in purchasing power after taxes and inflation.

Unfortunately, in today's interest-rate environment with low rates caused by the Federal Reserve's manipulation of them, it is a losing proposition for anyone with savings because, after taxes and inflation, their savings are losing purchasing power.

However, if things are this simple and the Federal Reserve is not manipulating rates, it might be easier to figure out which direction interest rates are headed. If the economy is doing well, then people will be willing to pay a higher price for goods and services, driving up inflation. Businesses will be making enough money from the markup of stuff that people are buying and will therefore be able to pay the higher rates banks are charging for loans. Banks can then pay a higher rate to depositors, giving them a positive, "real" rate of return.

If the economy begins to soften as in a recession, the demand for loans also softens, and banks drop the loan rate in order to continue attracting borrowers. Earning less, banks then have less money to pay depositors. But with demand for goods and services waning, the price for those goods and services would not be going up much if at all, and depositors could accept a lower rate of return from the banks and still have a positive real rate of return after taxes and inflation. So we can readily conclude that if the economy is strengthening, rates are likely to rise, but if the economy starts to soften, then rates should come down.

Now that we know it is the economy that *should* cause interest rates to rise and fall (growing economy = rate increase, softening economy = rate decrease), let's look at why the economy expands and contracts in the first place. This is commonly referred to as the "business cycle" and goes something like this. In an expanding or growing economy, business is good. Companies are supplying their goods and services, meeting the existing demand (supply and demand). They make profits and use these profits to increase their supply so they can sell more in the growing economy. They increase capacity and hire more employees. These employees, with their new jobs, add to the growing economy by buying goods and services from the companies that make up the economy, and the economy continues to grow.

Because companies are hiring, the demand for employees starts exceeding the supply of good employees—so businesses now have to compete for the limited pool of workers and must offer higher pay and more expensive benefits. In order for businesses to afford these rising costs, they increase the price of their goods and services. In a growing economy, these costs are easily absorbed because of the higher-paid workforce having more discretionary income, and business is good. As this growing economy *seems* like it will never end, they raise prices in an effort to increase profits, borrowing additional money to expand the size of their business in an effort to increase the supply of their goods and services.

Now their fixed costs have increased (new loan) but as long as their goods and services continue to sell at the higher prices, business is good. Unfortunately, everything has limits, including the economy. The supply of goods or services, therefore, starts to exceed the demand. In order to maintain the level of sales needed, the company now reduces the price of its goods and services in an attempt to make the same profit by selling greater quantities at a lower price.

At the same time, because of lower profits, they must take steps to make ends meet by cutting costs. One of these cuts is employees' salaries and benefits, and the company is forced to lay off workers. As the demand for jobs exceeds the supply, people are willing to work for less to compete for fewer jobs available. This reduces incomes, resulting in workers having less to spend and causing the economy to soften further.

Business is not so good. At the trough of the business cycle, the company costs to produce goods and services now exceeds what they can sell them for, and the company starts to cut production, laying off more workers in an effort to reduce losses. At some point, the supply for the company's goods and services drops so low that the demand, because of the enticingly low prices, starts to exceed their supply and prices stop falling. As demand persists, companies begin to increase supply and need to start hiring back employees. This is less costly to the company because employee demands for high wages and benefits are now overshadowed by their simple need for a job. While the economy is weak, the company can't raise prices, but the rehired employees' spending slowly strengthens the economy—and the cycle starts all over again.

Notice that the business cycle—trough to expansion, expansion to peak, peak to contraction, and contraction to trough—is rooted in human nature. From the company (which, of course, is run by people) to the employees, it is all a function of fear and greed. As the economy expands, the people running the company try to make more money (greed) by increasing capacity (increasing infrastructure and hiring more employees) and raising prices. When they go beyond what the economy can absorb, resulting in both sales and profits falling, fear sets in, and they rush to shed costs (employees) and reduce supply in order to minimize losses.

This same thought process goes for employees. As the economy grows and strengthens, companies are vying for good employees and workers demand more from the companies (greed), thus spending these higher incomes and improving their lifestyles.

As the economy softens, fear rules the day, and holding on to a job at any salary becomes the priority. People begin spending less and saving more for fear of losing their jobs and not having enough money to afford their fixed costs such as mortgage, rent, food and utilities.

Can you see now how simple this can be, conceptually anyway, and how easy it is to determine the state of the economy and where interest rates, the stock market, and real estate prices are headed? Being a part of the economy, whether as an employee or employer, you should be able to *feel* where the economy stands in its ever-repeating cycle and react accordingly.

Enter the U.S. government and the Federal Reserve.

Here's where it gets complicated, as I mentioned earlier, regarding the Federal Reserve's manipulation of interest rates. As the economy contracts, the government attempts to pick up the slack from the resulting decreased spending by the private sector (consumers and businesses). They do so by increased government spending and reducing taxes. Increasing government spending infuses the economy with much-needed money that the private sector stops spending during an economic downturn. Reducing taxes leaves more money in the pockets of consumers, allowing them to spend more than they would otherwise have to spend and thereby infusing cash into the economy—money that would not otherwise be available.

It doesn't end here. The Federal Reserve has a few arrows in its quiver when required to help an ailing economy. Remember, they set the banking reserve requirements and set the discount rate which is the rate that banks can borrow from the Federal Reserve, if necessary. But more important is the fact that banks use the discount rate to set the prime rate, typically at 3% above the discount rate.

Many other bank-lending rates are also tied to the prime rate. So if the Federal Reserve wants to stimulate the economy, they lower short-term rates by dropping the discount rate and also lowering the reserves which banks are required to hold, allowing them to loan out more of their deposits and inject more money into the economy at lower rates.

With the government setting fiscal policy (raising or lowering taxes and spending) and the Federal Reserve setting monetary policy (raising and lowering reserve requirements and short-term rates), how do we pinpoint where we are in the business cycle? It is difficult with both the Federal Reserve and government trying to level off the natural ebb and flow of the business cycle. Together, during a growth period, they can raise interest rates, reserve requirements and taxes, resulting in lower spending in an attempt to prevent overheating, often leading to a nasty contraction.

But when the economy is contracting, they do the exact opposite to help soften the blow and keep the contraction from being too severe—similar to what medicine does when you are sick. Medicine prevents you from becoming so ill that you need to be hospitalized. Unfortunately, the economy's medicine, or stimulus, often has side effects. Those side effects are typically an increased national debt and inflation.

The only way the government can lower taxes and increase spending at the same time is by going into debt. The government borrows money it is not collecting in taxes to spend into the economy. If you think about it, this makes sense because it is exactly what each and every one of us does if our incomes are reduced but we want to continue spending. We simply whip out that credit card and spend money we don't have. The government does the same thing. They issue bills, notes and bonds to borrow money from anyone and everyone who will buy these investments.

The U.S. government is currently the largest debtor in the world, owing approximately $18 trillion—trillion with a capital "T"—and increasing that debt by about $2.35 billion (with a "B") *every single day*. With a population of about 314 million, this debt represents about $57,300 per every man, woman and child in this country. But the problem isn't so much the government borrowing to spend in bad economic times as it is not paying the debt down during good economic times. Politicians become addicted to spending and can't seem to stop once spending is no longer needed to stimulate the economy. So the national debt just continues compounding.

On an individual level, if you and I borrowed money (credit cards, home equity loans, etc.) simply to make ends meet, we would eventually run out of credit and if nothing changed, end up unable to pay our debt payments, going bankrupt. The added benefit, however, of a sovereign nation, is that we as individuals don't possess the ability to print money. Imagine if after your credit ran out, you had the ability to walk down into your basement and simply print as much money as you needed to make ends meet. This is what the U.S. government does in conjunction with borrowing money on a regular basis. They issue new bonds, notes, and bills to pay for the old maturing bonds, notes and bills and to help make ends meet because of excess government spending.

When governments simply print money, it can cause an even greater problem—inflation. Without corresponding growth in the economy, each dollar in circulation becomes worth a little less with every dollar the government prints. This erodes the value of every dollar out there along with its purchasing power.

Inflation has been called a stealth tax. Taxes reduce directly what people have left to purchase goods and services. As inflation rises, people can't afford the same amount of goods and services even though they have the same amount of dollars to spend. The result of higher taxes or higher inflation is the same—that people are able to afford fewer goods and services. One problem with inflation is that people don't readily blame government for this as they do with direct taxation, which is plainly visible. It is therefore less noticeable and more palatable for politicians to vote for spending bills and increase the amount of debt the government can borrow rather than vote for a tax increase.

History is scattered with failed governments which have printed so much money out of thin air that it caused their currencies to become worthless. By the end of World War II, for example, it took a wheelbarrow full of German marks to buy a loaf of bread. By the time Rome fell, their gold and silver coins were only comprised of 2% gold or silver covering 98% lead, making them virtually worthless. Also, many Central and South American nations went bankrupt during the late 1900s after they borrowed more than they could repay. Then they printed so much money out of thin air that they actually destroyed their currencies. When no one any longer accepted their currency as having any value, they could no longer pay their debts—defaulting on all debt—and the investors holding that debt lost their investment. As it turned out, many of those investors were large U.S. banks.

This is the typical result of runaway inflation. However, even with relatively mild inflation over a long period of time, stable currencies like the U.S. dollar (the currency of the largest economy in the world) can suffer considerable erosion. Of note here is that during the 20th century, the United States had tremendous growth and evolved into the world's only super power—while at the same time the dollar lost over 95% of its purchasing power.

So how do we use this information to better figure out the current state of our economy and guess where it is headed? Well, as we've already determined, the only two institutions which have any direct impact on the economy in the United States are the government and the Federal Reserve; one having the ability to borrow, spend and lower or raise taxes and the other having the ability to set short-term interest rates and increase or decrease the money supply.

So if these institutions have the ability to impact the economy, exactly *how* do they do it, and what is their motivation? They collect more revenue (taxes) when the economy is robust. The more money changing hands, the more taxes collected. The more taxes collected, the more money the government can either spend or use to pay down debt, strengthening the country's balance sheet. Both are in the country's best interest.

So I think it is fair to say here that the government is prone to do whatever makes the economy more robust. The Federal Reserve's mandate is to provide for a safe, stable monetary and financial system and more recently, to maximize employment. But their role has also expanded throughout the years in an attempt to moderate the natural boom-and-bust swings in the economy caused by the business cycle. With this in mind, it is in the Federal Reserve's best interest to keep the economy in a Goldilocks state—not too "hot" which might be inflationary and not too "cold" which might be recessionary.

Now, knowing the motivations of both the Fed (Federal Reserve) and the U.S. government, we can make educated guesses as to what they may do depending where the economy is at any point in time. For example, if the economy is doing extremely well, the Fed may raise rates to slow it down and reduce the money supply in an effort to keep inflation from getting out of control while the government may slow down spending and pay down debt. Conversely, if the economy is heading into a slump, they might do the exact opposite to try and mitigate, to some degree, the downturn.

Sometimes the Fed's interests and the government's interest are at odds with one another. The government's interest would seem to be the ever-growing economy with less concern about inflation. One reason for this is because inflation is a debtor's best friend as long as it is not accompanied by high interest rates. The fact that inflation tends to make the dollar less valuable relative to other countries' currencies doesn't hurt either because it makes what we produce less expensive to foreign buyers (more competitive) and foreign goods more expensive here at home (less competitive).

This helps balance the trade deficit when we sell more and buy less collectively to and from foreign countries. Being the largest debtor in the world, inflation or the devaluing of the dollar's purchasing power allows the government to pay its debts back with less expensive dollars. Said another way, it reduces the value of the IOUs foreigners are holding, having invested in U.S. debt.

Here is a good example. The U.S. government prints money to pay for the Iraqi and Afghani wars which consequently causes the U.S. dollar to be worth less, forcing our creditors to help us pay for these wars. When the $1.25 trillion dollars the Chinese own of our debt becomes 10% less valuable in purchasing power, they in essence, contributed $125 billion toward the war effort. Unfortunately, the same goes for everyone in this country as well whose income and savings buy 10% less. Remember here that inflation is a stealth tax to anyone who owns or deals in dollars or dollar-denominated investments.

The Fed wants a more stable dollar but also a stable economy. The answer to a more stable dollar is to increase interest rates, making dollar-denominated bonds more attractive to investors. Increasing rates would also tend to slow the economy and reduce inflation. Unfortunately, if the economy is already in a downturn, increasing rates could push it over the edge into a free fall and undermine the Fed's objective for a stable economy. This is why the Fed has not been able to raise rates even though it wanted to.

So from a short-term perspective, it is unlikely that interest rates will rise in the near future. If they did the dollar would strengthen even further than it has been, making imports less expensive and ushering in deflation, which undermines the Fed and our government's efforts to create moderate inflation. What also seems to be moderating the impact of inflation, however, is a softer economy keeping the price of both non-essential goods and labor costs down.

From a long-term perspective, decades perhaps, it is in the government's best interest both here and abroad to keep rates as low as possible and inflation as high as can be tolerated—but without forcing interest rates up. As we discussed earlier, the reason for this is because inflation is a debtor's best friend. The national debts of most industrialized nations are motivation enough to keep rates low and inflation high, but the cost of the social programs most industrialized countries sponsor is problematic. In the U.S., the future costs of Social Security, prescription drugs and Medicare for the baby-boom generation will eventually dwarf the existing national debt by four times. Without inflation continually eroding those benefits, our government cannot continue to afford these programs on the backs of successor generations.

How does this happen? Social Security benefit checks increase annually with the CPI (Consumer Price Index). This index, however, excludes some of the biggest drivers of inflation—such as food and energy—and calculates other items in a way that lowers the CPI even further. If real inflation is running at 7% and the reported CPI goes up by only 2%, then the benefit is eroded by 5%. The compounding effect of this over many years is the only way it can be remotely affordable. Even if this occurs, it is likely that benefits will still have to be scaled back to a degree for some retirees. Either way, even if baby boomers get the amount they've been promised upon retirement, their money will buy significantly less than they ever imagined. This will force the baby-boom generation to put off retirement or work part-time well into retirement just to make ends meet.

This can be difficult to grasp. So let me try to illustrate the point. Let's say there is a 57-year-old who has 10 years to go before retirement. His current Social Security benefit is estimated to be $2,000. Ten years from now, compounding by 2% per year, this benefit will rise to $2,438. Let's assume the median income in America today is $51,000 and of that, the federal government collects 15.3% in Social Security and Medicare taxes, totaling $7,800 per year. In this example, it equates to about 3.9 months of the retiree's current benefit payment ($7,800/$2,000 per month = 3.9 months). If the median income compounds at the rate of real inflation, say 7%, then in 10 years it will rise to $100,325. Applying the same 15.3% tax rate, this would equal $15,350 which would pay 6.3 months of the retiree's benefit at that time ($15,350/$2,438 per month = 6.3 months) or almost 38% longer.

Who gets hurt in this scenario? Well, if incomes virtually double over 10 years, you can rest assured the cost of living will as well. That being the case, the $2,438 the retiree gets at retirement will only buy half that—$1,219 worth of goods in today's dollars, eroding his $2,000 benefit down to a current value of $1,000. In this case, baby boomers would be blindsided and totally unprepared financially to retire, regardless of how much they might like to. Retirement simply would not be an option for many. And with the prospect of people living longer, this problem will become more and more exacerbated.

The more socialistic countries of Europe will have even greater challenges and will have to cut expected benefits even more than the U.S. or allow inflation to cut deeper into their aging population's lifestyles. Either way, I don't see a viable scenario for decades to come, if ever, where inflation will be reined in globally.

If you accept this assertion, then you can invest accordingly for the long term by making sure whatever you invest in is likely, if not guaranteed, to increase in value over time along with inflation going up. What goes up with inflation? The same things that drive inflation higher. Stuff like commodities, real estate and stocks. These, however, don't tend to do well in a recessionary or contracting economy. This is why it's not only beneficial to psychoanalyze the economy but absolutely crucial if you want your investments to work as hard as you do and have a chance at providing the future lifestyle you are investing for. And sometimes the economic climate is such that not losing money or your investment principal is the best you can do. You have to decipher when the risk is simply too great. In higher-risk times like those we are currently facing, the return *of* your investment principal is more important than the return *on* your investment principal.

Caveat emptor!

6

STICK WITH FUNDAMENTALS

SO NOW THAT we have determined it is difficult to decipher exactly where we are in the economic cycle, how do we identify the risk and potential reward of different investment opportunities?

For over 30 years as a financial planner and investment advisor, I have walked my clients through the exercise of weighing risk and reward. To successfully accomplish this it is necessary to take everything you've learned so far and apply it to each potential investment, determining how that investment is apt to perform in the current and near-term economic environment. It is also necessary to factor in your time horizon—the number of years between now and when you will need to use this money you are investing. Finally, you have to give yourself a heavy dose of understanding that little, if anything, is guaranteed. Even U.S. treasury bills are only as good as the U.S. government backing them. And as highly unlikely as it may be for the U.S. government to default on those debts, it is *not* impossible. With this final caveat, you are ready to start weighing risk and the potential reward of various investments.

Passive investments are those you have little if any control over. Buying a publicly-traded stock falls into this category. You can analyze the company books, read the annual report and determine that the current economic environment is conducive to that company's business success—but in the end, you have no absolute control and need to trust the numbers on the balance sheet as well as the competence of the company's management.

The decisions management makes, the talent of their salespeople and purchasing agents and the potential sudden economic turns in that company's particular industry will determine whether or not the company whose stock you've invested in does well. Then, even if the company increases its profits, the market will ultimately determine whether the price of that stock goes up or down. If more people want to buy their stock in the future than want to sell, then the price will rise and vice versa. You can only make an educated guess based on the information available to you at the time and hope your reasoning is sound. But even then, you can't be *guaranteed* of a successful investment because you can't predict and factor in everything that might possibly happen to impact the stock of that company.

For example, let's say you invest in a company that builds infrastructure in developing nations. The company's debt is low, profit margins are high and costs are tightly controlled. The management is mature and has a proven track record for high performance. The P/E (profit-to-earnings) ratio is low from a historical perspective and the company is receiving good press. All conditions are positive for this company to do extremely well—until a border skirmish breaks out in one of the countries your company sells to and war is looming. Investors head immediately for the exits and start selling this stock as irrational fear grips the market. At the end of the day, week or month this stock could be down 20%, 30% or even 60%—all because of a risk that was totally unforeseen and probably unknowable when making the decision to buy the stock.

On the other hand, non-passive or active investments can have a degree of safety that doesn't exist in passive investments, that being your involvement. Your expertise in the investment, whether it be a business you control to some degree or a piece of managed real estate, can mitigate some of the risk. I emphasize "can" because too often enthusiasm for the particular enterprise blinds you to some of the risks inherent in the investment. Emotional involvement can often hinder the ability to properly and objectively analyze the risk. Too often, even a successful start-up endeavor can grow beyond the ability of the founder to manage it, making the investment much more prone to failure in the future as well.

Weighing the risk and potential reward of your investments should be an ongoing process, constantly applying new information that becomes available and can impact performance. Noticing fundamental changes such as the condition of the economy as a whole, the management of the company's stock you've invested in or the industry of your investment, is critically important. If the fundamentals you based your decision on have not changed, stick with your decision. Emotion can often rule the day for a short period of time but seldom, if ever, changes the fundamentals.

In our infrastructure stock example above, the potential of war breaking out in one of the countries in which the company you invested sold goods and services, caused an emotional and probably irrational selling spree. But this should really be looked at as more of a buying opportunity than a reason to sell because the fundamentals of your investment remain intact. The company is still well run and profitable, with the vast majority of the developing countries the company sells to still needing to build their own infrastructure. The fundamentals you based your original decision on have *not* changed—so you should stick with your investment because, over time, fundamentals will win out over emotions.

You may not realize it, but you are or should be weighing risk and reward constantly in most decisions, especially major decisions that may have nothing to do with financial matters. The decision to get married, for example, weighs marital bliss against the potential of an ugly divorce. After making the choice to marry, most couples at some point go through some speed bumps in the road that are often exaggerated by emotions. If they still love each other, then the relational fundamentals probably haven't changed, the problems can be worked out and usually are. However, if your spouse comes home one day and confesses love for someone else, then the fundamentals have probably changed, and it might be time to move on.

The decision to buy a house weighs the benefits and security of home ownership against the pressure of the added responsibility of paying for a mortgage and home maintenance. The decision to have children weighs the benefits of parenthood against the stress of child rearing. The decision of buying a new car weighs the benefits of comfortable, carefree transportation with the added debt of a car loan. Deciding to attend college weighs the benefits of that education followed by the hope of a higher-paying job against the years of hard work and indebtedness required to earn that degree. I could go on and on, but suffice it to say that most decisions start with weighing the inherent risks against the potential benefits based on the fundamentals or set of circumstances at a specific point in time. Those circumstances, like the fundamentals, can change and should be acted on accordingly when they do.

Leverage exaggerates matters. Whenever you invest in anything, leverage exaggerates the risk and potential reward. Let's say you have $100,000 to invest in real estate. Let me explain very simply what I mean here using two examples of how you might spend this $100k.

> **EXAMPLE #1.** If you use the $100,000 to buy a condo and rent it out, the numbers might look like this. The rent you receive is $1,000 per month and your expenses total $400 per month between real estate taxes, condo fees, insurance, etc. That nets you $600 per month or $7,200 per year which turns out to be 7.2% on your $100,000 investment. Therefore, your ROR (rate of return) would be 7.2% before tax considerations.

On the other hand...

EXAMPLE #2. Using the same $100,000, if you buy five similar condos as in the example above, using your $100,000 as the down payment (20%) and take out a mortgage for $400,000, spending a total of $500,000 and renting the condos out, the numbers might look like this. The rent you receive would be $5,000 per month with your expenses totaling $2,000 per month. That will net you $3,000 after expenses but before debt service or repayment. Assuming a $400,000 mortgage at 5% for 25 years, the principal and interest payment will be $2,339 each month, leaving you with a net take of $661 per month. That would be a cash-on-cash return of $7,932 on your $100,000 investment, which would be almost 8%—plus you own five times as much property. Sounds like an easy decision, right?

But look at what happens to these different investment examples above depending on whether prices for real estate rise or fall to see the added risk and potential reward that leverage adds. Let's assume the economic environment is such that real estate prices fell by 10%. In example #1, the value of your investment drops 10% and you lose $10,000. In example #2, however, because you own five times as much real estate, when the value of your real estate drops 10%, it represents a $50,000 loss or 50% of your original investment of $100,000. If real estate drops by 20%, the entire initial investment of $100,000 is wiped out. Without leverage, the likelihood of losing 100% of your investment is extremely rare.

On the flip side of the coin, the difference is equally substantial. If instead, real estate prices rise by 10%, the leveraged investor makes $50,000 on his $100,000 investment for a 50% return or doubles his money if real estate rises by 20%.

When dealing with investments in general, but especially in real estate, leverage changes the character of the investment from an *income* vehicle (unleveraged income real estate typically provides an income for the investor) to a *growth* vehicle where the investor is focusing on appreciation rather than income—which drastically increases the risk. The difference is similar between a growth stock (typically non-dividend paying and purchased for the potential appreciation in price) and a high-grade bond which is typically purchased for the dependable income it pays.

When determining whether to make an investment, as mentioned earlier, it is important to weigh the risk against the potential reward. For instance, if there's a chance you can lose your entire investment, there should at least be an equal chance of your doubling your money in the investment. I say "at least" because typically, you should only invest in something with greater earning potential than risk—but worst case, it should be equal. If at any point you feel the risk of an investment is greater than the potential return on it, then that might not be an investment you should make. At the very least, when risk is greater than potential reward, you need to understand that what you are really doing is gambling, not investing. Gambling may be fun but shouldn't be confused with investing and should only be done with money you can easily afford to lose. Whenever the odds are against you, it is probably best that you don't invest.

The greatest difficulty in evaluating whether to make an investment is in determining the odds or risk. The reason for this is rooted in human nature in our dual emotions of fear and greed, as these emotions tend to short-circuit the intellect.

Let me explain. If a clothing store you typically frequent is having a half-price sale, odds are you'll visit this establishment and buy something. If one gas station is offering fuel five cents cheaper than the next, that's the station you will pull into to fill up. It only makes sense. It's the reason we are drawn to "on sale" signs because we perceive a better value for our money.

When walking into the "investment store" we too often check our intellect and common sense at the door. It is typically when stocks are already high and heading even higher that we are excited to buy them, giving in to our greed. Conversely, when they have dropped in price, our fear prevents us from buying.

Taking this same mentality back to the clothing store, let's say that instead of a big "Sale" sign in the window the sign reads, "Sweaters on sale for twice the price of last week. Hurry in before they sell out!" Curiosity alone might draw some people to walk in and check this sweater "sale" out—but few, if any, will buy. However, let a stock double in price over the course of a week and it often creates a buying frenzy. But why? Shouldn't the same rationale hold true regardless what you are buying?

The late Sir John Templeton, a famous investor in the stock market, once said that when people are desperate to buy, then a good investor should sell, and when they are desperate to sell, buy. Seems accommodating, doesn't it? But this is the essence of buying low and selling high. It is the only proven formula throughout time immemorial. To do the right thing here, it is necessary to check your emotions at the door prior to walking into the "investment store" because the only time people are desperate to sell their stocks is when they fear losing even more than they have already lost, reaching their threshold of pain and unable take it any longer. Conversely, the only time people are desperate to buy is when a stock has gone up so high that the perception of even greater gain feeds their greed, creating a buying frenzy which bids the price well beyond any realistic fundamental value.

If a stock has an intrinsic value of say $10 and for whatever reason, is selling for $5, anyone would have to agree that the stock in question is a better value at $5 with less associated risk. After all, if it has already dropped 50%, how much *more* is it likely to drop? If that same stock were selling for $20, or double its intrinsic value, then most people would agree it has less potential (having already doubled) and more inherent risk where you could lose half your investment if the stock merely dropped to its intrinsic value.

The problem here is this. In evaluating the reason the stock is selling above or below its intrinsic or real value, it can't be argued that paying $5 for this stock isn't a better value (and therefore a better investment) than paying $20 for this same stock. The only reason people would buy this stock at $20 and not $5 is because of fear and/or greed—*neither* being a good reason to buy or sell. Hence, the finger of wisdom points back to Sir John Templeton's reasoning, although admittedly, it is still difficult advice to follow for most.

I summarize by suggesting a simple, common-sense approach to investing. Stick with fundamentals. Seek bargains like you would when shopping for anything—searching for quality at a sale price. The advice here is the same, whether looking to buy a sweater or making an investment.

7

SPIRITUALITY: NOT AT ODDS WITH CAPITALISM

LIKE MOST PEOPLE born in the U.S., I was raised in the Christian religion. The Bible teaches that it is as unlikely for a wealthy man to enter the gates of heaven as it is for a camel to squeeze through the eye of a needle—that it is better to give than to receive and that the poor will inherit the earth. Jesus lived on earth with no worldly possessions. He fed the multitudes, healed the sick, forgave the sinners and lived an otherwise selfless life. Many Christians around the world attempt to emulate his example as best as is humanly possible. But herein lies the proverbial rub: as best as is "humanly" possible. Every one of us is only human and therefore subject to the inherent foibles of human nature—self-preservation, greed, desire, fear, curiosity and all else prevalent to the human condition.

Being human, seeking financial growth and security and being Christian (or simply abiding by a culture that has its basis in Christian values) might at first seem incongruous. So how can we defend and take care of ourselves when we should be turning the other cheek and sharing with others to the point of personal poverty in order to inherit the earth in afterlife? How can we work hard and strive for a better life while not giving in to greed and the desire for worldly possessions which make our lives comfortable and our stomachs full? How do we refrain from being curious when it is curiosity which spawns investigation, experimentation, invention, innovation, cures for desease, etc., when we are supposed to have blind faith that God will provide? In addition, how do we have enough faith to keep from being fearful in our everyday lives?

Our fear of being hurt or dying motivates us to defend ourselves, not turn the other cheek. Our desire for comfort motivates us to work harder and acquire more. And it's tough to share with others and be charitable when the others in question choose not to work as hard as you do but desire the same comforts. It's also difficult to avoid criticizing those who choose not to strive to be all they can be and then ask for a handout—the tendency is to view these people as lazy or weak. Benevolent feelings toward others in such a case just seem to go against our human nature.

It seems our human needs and desires are tremendous motivators which push us forward—and isn't motivation a good thing? How do we reconcile these seeming dichotomies? Is God merely playing a game with his people, providing a blueprint for how he wants us to live but wiring us diametrically opposed to his teachings? Sometimes I envision God sitting up in heaven looking down on us just chuckling to himself, and other times he's in full belly laugh.

Let's take a closer look at all this, but before we do, I need to make certain assumptions, if you will, that I believe to be true. I need to point out what I believe to be universal truths. I believe God to be loving and not a god of death, hellfire and brimstone. I also believe there are natural consequences, both good and bad, for our actions, and that God *allows* those consequences to play themselves out—this is how we learn, especially if we choose not to take moral instruction to heart or learn by someone else's example.

Think of the child who is told not to touch the hot stove but does so anyway. When burned, he learns in one painful second that this is not a good thing to do. My guess is that this is how God may have attained his reputation with some for being a punishing, vengeful being—he allows us to live out the natural consequences of our actions.

I also believe that we humans have a spirit or soul, and it is this spirit/soul that separates us from all other life on earth. I also believe this spirit never dies, can't be destroyed, has no human or earthly bounds, transcends time and maintains our life's experiences with all the knowledge and love we've *ever* experienced and attained. We have all heard of and witnessed examples of how boundless the human spirit can be—and it *is*. All that we have, our potential and our free will to exercise that potential are gifts from God. He has given us much earthly instruction and if we follow his precepts, our lives will not only be better but more bountiful both spiritually and in this physical realm. This instruction comes in many forms, Christian teachings being only one of many.

What a mouthful, huh? Let's now address or reconcile what seem to be differences in what our culture or spirituality teaches us and what our human nature dictates.

Let's start with work. God gave us strong hands, strong backs and strong minds. So it would seem that using them is what God would want us to do. Therefore, there can't be anything wrong with hard work or the benefits derived from hard work. Taking this further, hard work often leads to great accomplishments, and it's only human to feel proud of those accomplishments and feel good when they are acknowledged by others—one of the benefits from hard work. Monetary success can also be one of those benefits.

So if there's nothing wrong with working hard and nothing wrong with great accomplishments, then there can be nothing wrong with the natural feelings of pride derived from them. Yet in our culture we are taught that neither excessive pride nor great wealth is a good thing. So either our cultural teachings are wrong or working hard and the benefits derived thereof are wrong.

Perhaps the truth (and the reconciliation) of these dichotomies lies between the two. Maybe pride *without* acknowledging where the ability of your accomplishment originates is what's wrong. It would seem that a loving God would rejoice in your accomplishments and you would have gratitude toward God for giving you the means. So maybe it's only when we take *total* credit for our accomplishments without giving credit to God that it is considered false pride—that the fault lies in not thanking God for the bountiful monetary blessings which are often an outcropping of our hard work. Acknowledging God's hand in our accomplishments also helps keep us humble—just a little side benefit.

How about fear and faith? Fear is a God-given emotion, an inherent part of our human nature, and yet the Bible teaches us to "fear not." Is our faith supposed to eliminate fear or is fear what God gives us to help us be cautious when it is appropriate to be so or to avoid things best avoided? What is blind faith and is taking this concept literally what God intended? I'm reminded of a joke about a person of great faith in God—John and a flood. When the forecast was for continuous rain and it was known that the residents of the town were going to be flooded out, the police drove around with megaphones calling for people to evacuate.

John, having faith that God would keep him from harm, chose not to evacuate. The flood waters rose, first above his car and eventually to his second-story window. A county sheriff's boat came along and the deputy asked him to climb in, but John refused, having faith that God would keep him from harm. The rain continued and the floodwaters rose until John was standing knee deep in water on top of his roof.

Suddenly, a Red Cross helicopter appeared. The pilot coaxed him to grab the rope ladder and be flown to safety—but again, John refused to take action, having faith that God would keep him from harm. So the flood waters rose further and John drowned. He arrived in heaven and asked why God had let him drown. God replied, "I sent the police with a warning, a boat to pick you up and a Red Cross helicopter to rescue you. What else did you want me to do?"

We must consider the possibility that fear might be God's way of warning us of danger prompting us to be cautious or avoid what's causing our fear. The "fear not" teaching could also be extolling the truth that what's eternal—the soul—is simply not subject to earthly peril and will always return to God unharmed, and *that* is what we should have faith in.

While here on earth, however, we have to reconcile our need for self-preservation and defending ourselves against evil or those who might want to harm us with the teaching of turning the other cheek. I don't believe God wouldn't want us to stand up against evil—quite the contrary. I also feel he would want us to defend ourselves against those who would do us harm.

Consider that an interpretation of this might be figurative rather than literal. Turning the other cheek could mean trying to look at the situation in a different way. It might mean simply that, in the course of defending ourselves and standing up for what is right, we should attempt to understand the motivation of people trying to do us harm and therefore try to solve the problem peacefully, if possible, before resorting to violence or force.

The reconciliation of these two seemingly opposing forces—our culture's teachings and our human nature—can be addressed both by seeking the truth in context behind the teaching and by understanding our inherent human condition and by realizing the two are not actually opposing forces but often require a broader understanding of the spiritual self within us.

Perhaps herein lies an answer which might help moderate the radical swings inherent to a capitalistic society. As I discussed in previous chapters, capitalism is balanced in a free society when people act in their own best interest. Maybe there would be less external balancing needed if there were more natural balancing done within the context of blending these cultural and spiritual teachings with our human nature.

For example, might the outcome have been different if the great industrialists of the nineteenth century—those who amassed incredible fortunes by, in part, exploiting laborers—demonstrated greater compassion for their employees? If they had blended the golden rule of "do unto others as you would have them do unto you" with their desire for the "pot of gold" so to speak, offering workers a fairer wage and providing more benefits, would there have been the need for unions? It is possible that doing the right thing by others in the pursuit of bettering life for oneself might have changed the outcome there.

Unions provided the external balance by representing laborers who joined together and acted in *their* own interests. Acting together as a union, workers forced employers to provide higher pay, greater benefits and better working conditions. But it was capitalism in a free society which allowed for the balancing necessary between early industrialists and their employees by empowering those employees to organize and act in their own best interest.

If early corporations and nineteenth-century industrialists had adopted greater foresight and *voluntarily* instituted the golden rule in the first place, this could have provided balance long before it was eventually forced into place. This balance would have been far less disruptive of business overall and avoided the tumultuous times and violence which too often coincided with the forming of early unions.

The same could be said today of the outrageous corruption and greed found on Wall Street and in corporate boardrooms. If balance were embraced and the interest of the company's owners, the stockholders, paramount in decisions made in corporate boardrooms across America and around the world, then there might be less need for excessive government regulation which will likely be the result of today's current greed and corruption.

I'm not a great believer in government intervention into free enterprise as it hinders growth, innovation and increased productivity, but I also find it difficult to justify the outrageous compensation packages bestowed on the CEOs of leading corporations, especially here in the United States. When the interest of those at the top who are running the corporations is so out of balance with the interest of the corporation's shareholders, then something needs to be done and will be. My contention is that the voluntary integration of the golden rule and our cultural teachings would be preferable to government regulation. But one way or another, balance will eventually be achieved. This is simply how capitalism in a free society works.

If we could just balance our spirituality with our human nature, balance the desire to achieve with a desire to do what's right, perhaps this might be what God intended with his various suggestions on how we should live and treat each other. I believe this two-pronged balance to be innate in all of us. Deep down, we recognize it. After all, isn't it the blend, the balance of our human nature with our spirituality, that creates the "human spirit" present in all of mankind?

8
IT'S ALL IN YOUR MIND—SO LOSE IT

COULD IT BE that we sabotage ourselves psychologically from acquiring wealth and financial independence? Our country was founded on Christian values, and those values permeate our culture regardless of whether you are Christian, of another faith, or no faith at all. We're a culture that believes in fair play, truth, respect for one another, charity, loyalty, fidelity and all that's perceived to be good. Many of our laws enforce the Ten Commandments, but even those commandments not enforced by the rule of law are enforced by public opinion and/or ridicule.

On one hand, we're taught that money is the root of all evil but on the other hand wealth is glamorized throughout the country and in the world. Somehow, we believe that people with money are inherently better than those without or at least we *often* think they are. As a nation, we are fascinated with wealth and the lifestyles of the rich and famous—after all, most of us don't have the mass media or paparazzi stalking our every move. We dream and fantasize about having wealth. Not only do we desire wealth, but we are also impatient in our quest for it. Instant gratification seems to be in our genes. This is why state lotteries are so successful and why casinos are such big money makers—and this is true in spite of the fact that every person who has ever stepped foot in a casino or ever bought a lottery ticket knows unequivocally that the odds of winning are extremely slim and that the vast majority of people lose.

So why do we gamble? Part of the reason behind gambling or hoping to make an instant killing is because the vast majority of people feel this is their only chance at becoming wealthy. Most people live paycheck to paycheck regardless of how substantial that paycheck is, spending much of their means on as much lifestyle as they can afford. The result is that they have very little money left (if anything at all) to build wealth, and even if they could put something aside, the process is so slow it's hard to stay disciplined, especially in our instant-gratification world. The process of building and acquiring wealth feels out of reach, impossible to most—so why bother even trying?

Adding weight to this justification is the money-is-evil culture kicking in which affirms it's better to be like everyone else, struggle all your life, do without and complain about the wealthy who think they are better than the rest of us. The mass media and our government help to vilify wealth by suggesting that the wealthy take advantage of the masses and that this is the very reason why they are wealthy and therefore deserve to pay higher taxes. There is an overriding belief that wealthy people *should* contribute vast amounts to charities to help the less fortunate. After all, they can afford it.

All of this serves to subconsciously repel wealth, sending a repeated message that we don't deserve to be wealthy or really don't want it. In addition, much of what keeps us from attaining wealth stems from our innate fears. The fear of rejection holds us back from asking for opportunities. The fear of failure prevents us from working on goals to reach our dreams. The fear of success prevents us from reaching our full potential because if we succeed, a precedent has been set, one that we will be expected to continue in the future, creating more pressure than many of us feel capable of handling.

Others simply have a view of themselves, a self-esteem view if you will, that doesn't allow for reaching and achieving beyond who they believe they are, their self-definition. In our own minds, we cling to a certain level of success that ends up defining us. This latter psychological fear, the fear of success, is both difficult to identify and comprehend. It is a roadblock I had to overcome myself as succeeding beyond my own "lot in life" was rooted deeply within my subconscious.

I was a $30,000-a-year real estate agent in my early twenties. Each year I earned $30,000 in commissions, not bad back in the early 1980s when the average price of a home was $40,000 to $60,000 with mortgage interest rates in the mid to high teens. Most years I was the top salesman second in earnings only to the 19-year office manager.

When I left real estate and entered a career in financial services, I continued to earn $30,000 a year, give or take a little. I was under-performing compared to my peers but seemingly working twice as hard. Then one day the firm I worked for brought in a psychologist, a sales coach of sorts, who taught the staff about subconscious fears that might be preventing us from reaching our full potential. Ultimately, this training revealed a classic "fear of success." It was identified that, once I hit my self-proclaimed, subconscious "limit" of $30,000 per year, I would begin the process of sabotaging myself, preventing myself from making any more. Once I became aware of what I was doing subconsciously and realized just how I was sabotaging myself, I stopped the self-defeating cycle—*doubling* my income the following year.

Throughout high school, my dream of success was to become an architect and earn that magic number of $30,000 a year. At that time in our country's economic history, a yearly income of $30,000 bought a handsome lifestyle. My divorced mother raised four children on a waitress's income and we never had much, reinforcing in my mind the dream of a $30,000 income. Even though double-digit inflation during the '70s eroded what $30,000 could buy, this figure remained stuck in my subconscious. So once I reached this dream of $30,000 annually, in my mind, I was all I could be. Anything beyond this self-proclaimed ceiling I dismissed as being well-off (if not wealthy)—an amount which someone of my stature in life neither deserved nor could attain.

Family and friends can also hold us back subconsciously, not necessarily by what they do or think but by what we are preconditioned by culture to *suspect* they might do or think. We all desire acceptance, especially from friends and family. This is one of those human conditions most in our society share—the fear of rejection by those we are closest to because they might no longer relate to us after we acquire more money or possessions than them.

Have you ever felt embarrassed by having more than your friends and family—embarrassed to share the news of a promotion or increase in pay? Have you ever harbored a reservation to tell your friends about an extravagant purchase made or expensive gift you received? If yes, why?

Shouldn't we feel free to share our successes and the enjoyment of the fruits of these successes with those we love the most? Or are we afraid they may become jealous and judge us, thinking we are now better than they are? Often, that old American culture starts creeping into our psyches, making us feel guilty for being successful and enjoying the benefits of that success. This is why many of us make an effort to downplay our successes, referring to them as luck or nothing more than good fortune.

Consider the following scenario. You win a car or luxury trip which others deem beyond your means. As soon as someone compliments you on the new car or oohs and aahs about the trip, are you quick to say how you won it and that you couldn't actually afford anything this nice because, after all, you are just like them? Heaven forbid you rise above your lot in life and the financial level of your friends and family for fear they will begin looking at you differently, judging you. Some might simply explain this as modesty, but whatever you call it, this mindset holds you back subconsciously from achieving all you're capable of in life.

Further evidence of this prevalent wealth-suppressing syndrome is the preponderance of self-help gurus, books and videos promoting the need to *visualize* ourselves as being successful, wealthy or whatever else we want to be before we can actually make it happen. In essence, the message here is that we have to reprogram our minds and change the thoughts preventing us from being all we can be because of the cultural programming of our minds that our culture unwittingly imposes on us from birth to adulthood.

Even further evidence of this point is that wealth seems to beget wealth. Admittedly, some of this is simply wealth being passed down through the generations, but if this were all there was to it, even vast family wealth would dilute to mediocrity within a few generations of irresponsible spendthrifts. I believe it is more than this in most cases. Being born into wealth appears to eliminate much of this fear of success and the resulting self-sabotage we've been discussing.

Instead, success and wealth are expected, not something out of the ordinary or something to be embarrassed about. People born into wealth, even moderately so, tend to see the human condition as limitless, restricted only by their own imaginations and creativity. They take advantage of whatever is available, often achieving with relative ease what most of us only stand back and marvel at.

There is something to the following sayings: "If you want to be wealthy, surround yourself with wealthy people." "If you want to be successful, surround yourself with successful people." "If you want to be a great ball player, play ball with great ball players." The point? We tend to *rise* to the level of those with whom we associate, again in part because of our need for acceptance.

The converse is also true. We tend to *drop* to the level of those we associate with, and therefore poverty tends to beget poverty. Is it any wonder your parents ridiculed you for hanging around with your "loser" friends, encouraging you to hang with better people? You may not have understood why at the time or agreed with them, but it was sound advice nonetheless.

Thinking back on my own life experience, I believe I rose through the psychological ranks by applying this principle. As a child, we couldn't afford to go out to eat much so I became a waiter and surrounded myself with people who could, even if I were simply waiting on them. With my mother never able to afford a home while I was a boy, as a young adult I surrounded myself with people buying homes even if I was simply selling them a house. And never dreaming I could attain wealth or financial security, as a financial planner, I surrounded myself with people who had attained relative wealth and financial security even if I was simply helping them manage it.

It was then, however, that I realized how ignorant most people are about money and investments (and I use the word ignorant in the literal sense here, meaning "without knowledge"). Although the people I worked with might have possessed a certain brilliance in ability or intellect in a particular field allowing them a degree of wealth and financial security, they did not understand what it took to turn that success into financial *independence*—financial independence being the ability to live the lifestyle you've grown accustomed to without ever again having to worry about how to afford it.

This makes financial independence extremely hard to quantify, however, because individual lifestyles vary tremendously. Some people have lived a lavish lifestyle and no longer have much need for the monetary pleasures in life. They've come to better appreciate the simpler pleasures that no amount of money can buy. Others have lived extremely comfortable lifestyles and want to maintain this level of comfort. Still others have never lived without the worry of their financial situation and yearn for the day they can alleviate those worries. And finally, many others have never experienced a lifestyle beyond mere necessities but are very content to live out their lives this way. We are all wired differently, and therefore wealth and financial independence are relative.

So in the final analysis, relativity has much to do with how we *think* and *feel* from a financial point of view. But there is so much more—relativity forms the basis of how we look at every aspect of our lives and is why I've devoted the next chapter to this important phenomenon.

9

EVERYTHING'S RELATIVE

WHAT DOES RELATIVITY have to do with capitalism, finance, economics and wealth? Wasn't that Einstein's theory having something to do with light and time—or was it something to do with the Big Bang theory? In any case, it's important to understand that absolutely everything is relative and the more you embrace this fact, the more content you will be.

Huh? Trust me and read on.

Envy, jealousy, and desire are just a few of our normal, human conditions. Most of us don't consider these positive qualities, but they are often motivating factors to great personal achievement. We all desire love, time, money and comfort, among other things. Wouldn't we all love to have someone who's madly in love with us and us with them—having plenty of time to spend together and also time to pursue what we want to do alone? And then of course, we'd want plenty of cash to acquire whatever pleasures and comforts we desire. Then surely life would be perfect...until it wasn't.

What do I mean here? Let's start with lover boy—or girl. Let's assume you are a woman who has just found the love of your life and he loves you just as much in return. That "as much" is relative and is determined by your past experience. Let's assume you are coming from a history of several relationships that, shall we say, were less than perfect. One was with a guy who was handsome and had a great physique—but was extremely self-centered, narcissistic, lacking in compassion and warmth, expected to be doted on and only really liked how you enhanced *his* image. Another may have been a guy who was just the opposite, not so good-looking, out of shape and with little respect for himself. Maybe he lacked motivation and wasn't very successful, so much so that he'd have to borrow money from you to him pay his cable bill—because he was too lazy to go out and get another job after being laid off from his previous one— for being too lazy to do that job. But man, did he think you were special. He even borrowed money from you to buy you flowers. How sweet. A real keeper, huh?

Now taking this what-if scenario even further, let's say this new guy had been involved with his childhood sweetheart who, in his opinion, was perfect in every way. In fact, they had plans to be married when she was suddenly hit and killed by a truck. He grieved the appropriate period of time and then met you, falling deeply in love.

Based on your different backgrounds, I would guess you are going to be a little more forgiving than he might be because of what you were used to in previous relationships—those being far from perfection, a very relative term in itself. So relatively speaking, this new guy is a dream. His view of a relationship and you, however, might be difficult to live up to because of what he previously experienced—she being the love of his life, and what he has come to expect as the standard. As his lofty expectations become annoying and you don't quite measure up, a little luster might slip from the relationship.

At that moment, both of you might still be together, but you now find yourself watching another couple walk hand in hand, gazing adoringly into one another's eyes and seeming so much in love. You enviously wish this were you, and yet even with all its little annoyances, *your* relationship is the envy of your poor girlfriend who just endured a nasty divorce, is now alone and full of anger and hate. Everything's relative.

Next let's consider the time you crave with this new love of your life and the time desired for activities pursued on your own as well. Assume you are the typical nine-to-fiver, five days a week. You walk out the door around 7:30 each morning, commuting to the city and arriving at work by 8:30 a.m. You leave the office later that day at 5:00 p.m., returning home at 6:00 p.m. So it is safe to say that the bulk of your free time is nights and weekends. You envy that attractive young woman in the next department over who leaves work around 2:30 p.m. every day—and has Fridays off—plus your boss seems to come and go whenever he pleases.

What you don't know is that the young woman whose schedule you envy made a deal with the boss to arrive at work early, by 6:00 a.m., in order to leave by 2:30 p.m. so she can meet her little boy's bus after school each afternoon. Complicating matters, her husband leaves for work at 2:00 each afternoon, working the second shift until midnight. They barely see each other, and she works as a waitress Saturday and Sunday nights to help make ends meet. Between yard work, house cleaning, grocery shopping and errands there is little time for her and her husband to spend together, and seldom, if ever, time alone. It might surprise you to know that this young woman envies the time *you* have, your free nights and weekends. Again, everything's relative.

As for your boss, he's the typical high-level executive. He begins his work day extra early, running in and out of the office throughout the day for meetings with customers or venders. He also stays late, brings work home on weekends and spends much of his Sundays planning for the next week. His wife and kids wish he had your schedule—everything's relative.

Now we come to wanting the money necessary for you to afford all the comforts of life. Well, how much is that exactly? You could easily quantify that amount of money, basing it on your current situation in life. If you are living on $50,000 per year, then

$150,000 per year would certainly allow you to live more comfortably. But once you get used to the bigger house, that newer nicer car and more extravagant lifestyle, this becomes your point of reference—and $150,000 is no longer enough.

You no longer think in the realm of a $50,000 lifestyle. Driving ten-year-old cars, living in a rental and eating in 29 out of 30 nights a month is no longer an option, and to do so would now be considered cruel and unusual punishment. You now require $150,000 just to be "okay." At this point it might take $300,000 to afford that more comfortable lifestyle.

People of lesser means look at those with more and can't imagine they might be living paycheck to paycheck as well, but often times they are. You can prove this to yourself by calling a realtor and asking him about the reasons those million dollar plus homes are selling. If honest with you, they would say it's because the residents of those homes have lived beyond their means, trying to outdo the "Joneses" and can no longer afford the home.

Few take pity on people in this situation because it is of their own doing, but when you are making a lot of money, relatively speaking, it's very difficult to live a far more modest lifestyle than you can easily afford. And yes, again, everything is relative. How many people earning $250,000 per year would live in a $250,000 fixer-upper of a home when they could easily purchase a $700,000 to $800,000 home? Find me that person and I'll show you the next "millionaire next door" or a person whose priorities vary widely from the mainstream.

Most of us don't understand how everything is relative until we've lived long enough to experience enough firsthand situations where we've been on two sides of an issue and are therefore able to understand both sides. One example of this is in politics regarding conservative and liberal points of view. When we are young and have little we tend to be more idealistic and liberal thinking. As we get older and start acquiring wealth (to whatever degree), paying taxes and realizing that every liberal handout costs money, many of us tend to become more conservative-minded. Then as we grow older, we either need more social assistance from government programs and morph to a more liberal mindset again, or we become well-off and can more readily afford to have a more liberal-minded attitude. We tend to alter our perspective based on our *own* self-interest. And where have we heard this before? My own life is an example of this long lesson in relativity, both financially and with relationships.

When young and foolish, or certainly when I was young and foolish, you sort of assume that once married, life would be like in the movies, the happily-ever-after thing. Unfortunately, that just isn't how it works, and in my case, my first marriage ended after seven years. Without getting into details, suffice it to say that my divorce wasn't much fun.

Two years later, however, I met the love of my life. Within a year we were married, and it's been marital bliss ever since. And if you believe that, I have some swampland in Florida I'd like to show you. But seriously, all kidding aside, my wife and I have a great marriage, but I don't believe my current relationship would have been this good if I hadn't experienced my first failed marriage. I could never have appreciated a normal loving relationship because it's what I always expected, and having had a marriage that was anything but that the first time around made me far more appreciative and grateful for what I have now. I probably have what many other married people have but for the reason mentioned, to me it's more special, and because of the appreciation on both our parts, I'm sure it's a stronger marriage than it might otherwise have been.

Financially, having come from a broken home with my mother supporting four of us on a waitress's pay, as I mentioned earlier, we seldom had extra and never owned our own home. I guess that's why it was so important for me to buy my first home at such an early age as soon as I was able to afford it. Like most first homes, that home was a "starter" and in a starter-home community.

Now I live in an average home in an upper middle class community, and albeit modest, it's a nicer home than I ever expected to own. Comparatively, it looks like the gardener's house for neighbor's 5,000 square foot mini mansion, but it's comfortable and we appreciate what we have. What might have been a wee bit small when we had three kids running around is perfectly spacious now that the kids are grown and living on their own. Again, everything's relative.

It seems the more success people achieve, the more that level of success feels normal—resulting in an even greater level of desired success desired to feel successful again. Sometimes all it takes is reflection, appreciation and a little gratitude. There's always going to be someone who has more and someone who has less, but everything being relative, is an important reality to acknowledge.

We all put our pants on one leg at a time. We all desire the same things. It's our level of satisfaction, contentment and tranquility that is subject to differing levels of success, wealth, health, time and people to love and share our lives with. The key here is appreciating what you have, where you are in life and trying to focus on what's really important. There is no satisfaction in constantly striving for the next level of success if you don't enjoy the level already achieved.

It is important to remember that getting to that next level always has a price. Your desire to provide more for your family may have been what drove you to that next level, but if you had asked them, they may have actually preferred more of *you* and less of what you brought home in the way of comforts and wealth. Often, as we grow older, it's only time which becomes the most precious commodity, but the great art of balance between working for income and enjoying quality time is what too many of us find challenging. It's for this reason that I've dedicated the next chapter to this topic.

10

PRIORITIES AND THE FINE ART OF BALANCE

THIS IS PROBABLY the most important chapter in the book and possibly the most difficult practice for humans to master. Achieving balance requires constant effort, reflection and awareness, but is certainly one of the more important accomplishments in life. Without it, we lose perspective and miss out on much of what life has to offer. It is notable that few people proclaim on their deathbeds that they should have spent more time at the office.

In defining a successful life, I describe one that is keenly balanced and directed by someone who is constantly aware of what's most important in life, someone who is able to prioritize properly at all times without having to obsess over the balancing act itself. This would be a "perfectly balanced life" and hence, a successful life. Fortunately, absolute perfection is not required to be happy and content—but the more balance, the better.

Like everything else, balance is relative. For the workaholic, spending a day over the weekend doing something other than work adds balance—just as some yard work does for the couch potato. Too much of anything is often unhealthy. I refer here to a full-spectrum meaning of health; physical, spiritual, psychological, and emotional. Each of these categories is intimately connected to the other.

Physically, there is much to achieving balance—from eating, to exercise, to managing stress and getting enough sleep. The body is an incredible, complex organism that can take a lot of abuse but performs *best* with balance. If we give our bodies the proper balance, not only do we feel better and lead much healthier lives, but we might also live to be 150 years old.

What would this require exactly? There are a great number of books written about every aspect of physical health, and it would be a daunting task to cover even a small fraction of the information available. The point is that we need a basic awareness of everything our bodies need to make them work well. Then we have a better chance at living healthy, happy, productive lives.

Our bodies need the right blend of vitamins and minerals. Unfortunately, because of over-farming the land and chemical fertilizers, our food supply no longer contains as many nutrients as it once did. So we often need supplements to supply our bodies with the proper amount of vitamins and minerals. The right balance of nutrients is also key. Too little or too much of one vitamin or mineral can be problematic, but all vitamins and minerals play a role in good health.

Vitamin D, for example, is important in that it helps build strong bones. In my experience, however, D has never been as exciting as the B vitamins which increase energy or vitamin C that helps prevent colds, or even vitamin E which helps with stamina. But more recently, new scientific evidence shows that vitamin D is linked to moods. Supposedly, D is a major building block for the body to produce the hormone calcitriol, which in turn helps the body create the hormone melatonin—a mood enhancer—and this is only one example of how our physical health chemically affects emotional and/or psychological health, another link in the balance.

Another example of how our physical well-being impacts our emotional and psychological health is exercise. Strenuous physical activity causes adrenaline secretion, the body's natural feel-good "drug." Typically, exercise increases your metabolism because the body requires more energy as a result of the physical exertion and often metabolizes fat to acquire the energy needed to keep you active. Conversely, the lack of exercise decreases your metabolism, resulting in your body needing less energy, and causing the excess calories ingested to be stored as fat. The more fat stored, the lower your metabolism tends to be, making it easier and easier to pack on the pounds. Obesity is the end result, and we all know the myriad of health issues associated with that.

Can we exercise too much? Sure. Again, too much of anything is typically not a good thing. But to answer this question, let's assume that the time it takes to exercise does not interfere with your otherwise well-balanced life. If this excess of exercise is building too much muscle, then it could be putting undo strain on tendons, ligaments and cartilage that can be problematic later in life. If the excess exercise is all cardio, you could not only be straining joints but also addicting the body to the dopamine excreted from long cardio sessions that delivers a high and can give you the blues when taken away. As you can see, *excess* is typically not a good thing regardless of what it is that's excessive. There's a saying that has stood the test of time: "Everything in moderation." It's one of those universal truths that is good to live by. Even alcohol in moderation has been shown to have health benefits.

Can we eat too little? Sure, even though the human body actually requires far less food than most of us eat. However, eating too little causes the body to start using stored energy—first in the way of stored body fat but then by using up muscle tissue, which is extremely unhealthy.

We've touched on the emotional and psychological as they are impacted by the physical but what about the other way around? Stress-related ailments and disorders are said to be the reason for 75% to 90% of doctor visits. Chronic acute stress contributes to an out-of-balance biochemistry with elevated cortisol and suppressed serotonin which then lead to both mental and physical health problems. Simply put, stress makes us more susceptible to all forms of disease from diabetes and heart disease to cancer.

A lack of balance can have catastrophic consequences in other psychological areas as well. A constant barrage of violence in our culture whether it be from TV, movies or video games has made people, especially young people, more accepting of real-life violence and more prone to violence themselves. The end result is a lack of respect for and appreciation of human life. The ripple effects of this are many. Too many children grow up with little respect for each other, for authority, for life in general and ultimately, themselves.

Pornography, soft porn and sexual exploitation throughout our culture have a similar effect on our lack of appreciation and expression of love for one another as well as lovemaking. Romance, too, often takes a back seat to sex, rather than romance leading to love- making. This ultimately makes the sexual act less fulfilling, making us feel less loved, less cared for. The yearning for satisfaction in these areas can then lend itself to searching outside of marriage and infidelity.

The culture bombards us with excitement, action and constant stimulation. Our senses are on overload. The greater the stimulation, the less satisfaction that stimulation provides and the more we crave to feel stimulated again. Is it any wonder then, that just to get our attention, horror movies have become more horrific, comedies funnier, sports more extreme and the emotional charge of violence or sex now central to most advertising?

If you question this, rent an old horror flick or comedy. If you are younger, you will find the movies boring. If old enough to remember these movies, you'll be surprised by the transformation that has taken place within this venue. You will also be amazed at your underwhelming reaction to these old movies now versus the feeling you recall when you watched them originally.

Many of us experience this same excitement and stimulation on the job. The feeling of satisfaction in accomplishing something, finishing a task, makes it difficult for many of us to simply relax and do nothing, especially when our fortunes are tied to the success of the company or work we do. Regardless, we still need balance in all facets of our lives. Our minds need peaceful down time, the simple pleasures of playing a board game, taking a walk or listening to music—not a constant barrage of overstimulation. We need quiet time with the ones we love. We also need time alone to pursue hobbies and sports or to enjoy simple reflection on where we are in our lives. Each of us needs time to get back in touch with who we are and what is really important. With the demands on our lives coming at us from all directions, prioritizing personal time becomes as important as prioritizing our other daily and weekly activities.

It's very difficult to maintain balance because many needs in life cry out in competition, demanding our attention. How many of us, in the middle of a conversation, answer our cell phones immediately? What makes the person on the other end of the phone more important than the person sitting in front of you? Often these demands for our attention can't be ignored—like a baby crying or a danger warning—but many times they can be ignored and should be.

One of the modern advances in the balancing act of life is the opportunity to work from home. Years ago, when my wife and I were looking for a house, we thought to incorporate a home office in our search because I was tired of working so hard and never seeing my family. Working from home was also more cost effective than renting office space outside the home. After that, instead of calling to say I'd be working late and wouldn't be home for dinner, I simply took a break, joined my family upstairs for dinner and then returned to my downstairs' office for a few more hours to finish my day's work—a healthier life option emotionally and financially.

Working from home offered the flexibility to sit with my daughter as we waited for the school bus each morning. It allowed me a last-minute run with the lunch one of the kids forgot to put in a backpack, or pick one of them up from the nurse's office when not feeling well. It allowed me the flexibility to be more of a dad while continuing to provide a good living for my family. It gave me and millions of others working from home more balance in our lives. Not everyone can do this but those who can have a big leg up in this proverbial pursuit of balance.

Emotionally, the benefit of balance in our lives is powerful. By making time for family, friends, and ourselves we feel more complete. We feel a sense of community, of belonging, and a part of something bigger than ourselves. Spending time with and being around people we care about makes us feel nurtured and loved in return. This sense of wellbeing crosses over to the physical and psychological, ultimately enhancing our mental and physical health as well.

Finally, we need to balance our physical lives with our spiritual lives. I'm not simply talking about making time to attend church or temple which relates more to our religious *practices*. Spiritual lives are about *relationship*—the direct connection to our maker, our inner spirit, our God. We've heard it said that there is no atheist in a foxhole, and this speaks to a driving spirit within that surfaces unexpected and unbidden. Few living on earth amidst balanced ecosystems—systems which create the perfect environment for life or showcase the miracle of the human body in all its frailties and complexities—believe this simply to be happenstance.

The spiritual transcends the physical, and most feel or sense that we are more than mere flesh and bone. This is why I feel spirituality is something desirable that we should consider and seek to integrate into the balancing of our lives.

There's so much to balance, but the more successful you are in the fine art of balance, the richer your life will be. *The ultimate success story is a well-balanced life.*

11

MEN & WOMEN, VENUS & MARS, SECURITY & LIVING IN TENTS

NOW IF I may, let me pull you out of the clouds from that well-balanced and spiritually-conscious life back to how the sexes differ in their views and perception of money, investments and business.

First let me state that there are no absolutes between the genders financially. There are financially savvy, risk-taking women just as there are head-in-the-sand, ultra-conservative men and everything in between and on both sides of the gender coin. This chapter will talk in generalities about the sexes—always a dangerous approach in the sense that ruffled feathers by either sex often result from this type of generalizing. Having made the above-referenced disclosure that I fully acknowledge both sexes have the ability to define their own attributes outside these generalizations, let's begin.

It's been my experience over the past 30 years of my financial planning practice to note that women are typically more financially conservative than men. Aside from gambling problems (a separate topic not applicable to this chapter or book) men tend to be willing to accept more risk than women. This difference can be problematic for both, with men being seen as too reckless and women too cautious. So my first exploratory question here is why might this be the case?

Can the reason be found when we revert to yesteryear when women were dependent on men—the time in history when men handled all finances in the household as well as business matters, and there were few if any women in the workplace let alone corporate finance? Perhaps it's a natural consequence from centuries of specific social behavior and acceptance. Why men and women respond differently with regard to money and finances might be interesting to ponder, but what is important to this discussion is how this difference *manifests* itself and what each sex stands to learn from the other in the disclosure.

Let's begin with men. Not only are men typically willing to take on more risk than women, but they also have a tendency for less due diligence prior to investing, perhaps because they feel if the investment is lost they could always sleep in a tent and start over—or maybe it's for the same reason men don't ask directions. Who knows? But it is best to understand as fully as possible the investments you're making before parting with your hard-earned money.

Women, on the other hand, tend to take more time to understand what they are investing in. However, they too often let fear or lack of *complet*e understanding prevent them from taking an otherwise acceptable level of risk needed to acquire an investment with a potentially higher return.

This difference between men and women is magnified in small businesses and could be part of the reason why many fail during the first year. So in an effort to clarify an understanding between the sexes as it relates to money, let me spend a little time on this topic.

When starting a business or new venture, it's important to do your homework. Both a business plan and extensive research are essential with start-ups in order to overcome the odds of failing. However, once a man understands the concept of the business or venture, he's more likely than a woman to invest his time and money without understanding *every* detail. The down side here is that missing a crucial detail can derail a new business early on. But sometimes moving ahead can be a good thing because if people wait for every detail to be made known prior to opening a business, fewer business start-ups would take place. On the other hand, if a woman, in her typically more cautious approach, gets lost in all the details and the myriad of potential problems a new business can face, the trigger might never be pulled, resulting in an opportunity lost. There is something to be said for grasping the overall business concept and then dealing with the details as they arise. As we learned in the last chapter, balance is key in taking the plunge to begin a new business.

The start-up process can be challenging enough on its own, but when adding partners into the mix, a new business can become nearly impossible. When dealing with a partner, the human relationship and personality issues become part of the mix, and must be worked through in addition to the business concept itself. Those issues should be ironed out, agreed on and put in writing before any business or venture is launched. If not, over time these issues will most likely derail the business even if it would have been otherwise viable.

Perspectives vary because everyone is unique and from different backgrounds and therefore views key issues differently. Some people work hard and others hardly work. Some people are detail-oriented and others conceptual. There's an old saying about partnerships: always have an odd number, and three are too many. People in general, but men especially, are inclined to assume that a friendship/social relationship will automatically make a good business partnership. Certainly, some of the aspects that go into a partnership exist in a social friendship, such as liking one another and trust, but that's about where it ends. Just because you're friends with someone, doesn't mean you can work together successfully. And when you think about it, the very fact that you are friends probably means you have much in common—which doesn't necessarily translate into a good partnership. It's best to have a partner who has strengths where you have weaknesses and vice versa, two pieces completing the puzzle.

If you need partners in a business venture, outline ahead of time who will do what, when and for how much. Brainstorm every possible scenario you can think of in an attempt to anticipate challenges that could arise or situations that might go wrong. Then determine exactly how these potential situations will be handled. For example, what will happen if one partner changes his mind and wants out only months into the business? Or, heaven forbid, what will happen if a partner dies—will the remaining partner(s) then be in business with the deceased partner's spouse or heirs, people they may not even know? Before starting a business or venture, you need an ending strategy much like determining what might be cause for a divorce before committing to marriage. This is sage advice whether you are a man or a woman.

According to various studies, another difference between men and women in business is in their applied ethics. One study found that men tend to apply ethical principles egocentrically, meaning that if the outcome of an ethical decision impacts the man negatively, he will likely perceive the entire situation as unethical. However, if the projected outcome might have a positive impact on him personally, then this is more likely to overshadow any unethical aspects of the decision. According to these same studies, women tend to be stricter in the application of ethics involved in a decision, regardless of its outcome, perhaps the reason more companies are placing more women on their boards.

A study conducted by Terry Odean, a University of California professor, found that women outperformed men when investing in stocks by 1.4% to 4.6% (depending on the particular study). Odean concluded the reason for this difference in success is related to "overconfidence in men when pushing forward in their decision-making." This coincides with my conclusion that men in general are willing to take greater risk than women without the prerequisite amount of due diligence.

To summarize, you should understand as much as possible the investment, business or business venture you are looking to invest in. But women should be careful not to overdo the analysis as this can lead to paralysis. It is also valuable for women to restrain empathetic tendencies and keep the decision-making process more business-like, avoiding the likelihood of others taking advantage of them. Men, on the other hand, should engage in more homework and greater analysis of the proposition. And once a decision is made, men should step away briefly, allowing a cooling-off period before finalizing the transaction. After this brief pause, they should reassess the situation. If their buying decision still makes sense, then take the plunge. This process will help short circuit men's natural tendency to ignore the risks and jump in too soon.

Remember, regardless of what the PC crowd insists, men and women come to the decision-making table with inherent differences. Recognizing this will not only make you a better investor but also more successful in relationships, both business and personal.

12

POLITICS:
THE GOOD, THE BAD AND THE UGLY

YOU MAY BE asking why political beliefs have anything to do with finances, investments or capitalism in general. Allow me to explain. We live in a free society and yet few appreciate those freedoms, how they were achieved and how they are maintained. Most of us enjoy these freedoms but don't fully appreciate them. If we did, more citizens would vote and then pay closer attention to what the elected politicians are actually doing once in office. We seldom think about this, but the politicians we vote into office affect our investments and every other aspect of our financial lives—from the taxes we pay to how much the dollar buys or doesn't buy, as the case may be, to how much and when we will receive Social Security.

When politicians vote to raise taxes, we have less money to spend on ourselves and our families. When they create money out of thin air by simply printing it, our dollars typically buy less and we have to spend more to afford the same lifestyle we enjoyed in the past. We then have to spend more time working for that additional money because our paychecks seldom go up as fast as the cost of those things we want to buy in order to maintain our current lifestyles.

So it comes down to making more or doing with less. Being more diligent in monitoring what our politicians are doing would bode well for all, but who has the time when we are all working so hard to make ends meet?

Most of us feel helpless to effect change at the government level, so apathy sets in and political concerns remain out of the mind of the average citizen. Statistics show that only 60% of eligible Americans bother to vote in a presidential election. The voting percentage in non-presidential elections drops from there, and our local election's turnout is the most dismal of all unless there is a controversial issue up for a vote. This is both good and bad. It's good if those who do not bother voting are clueless as to what or for whom they would be voting. It's bad in that too many of us fall into this category. It's also unfortunate that too many vote without knowing the substance of issues on the ballot.

Not to excuse apathy, but most of us simply don't believe our one vote matters or makes a difference in any way. We all agree that hundreds, thousands or millions of votes matter collectively—but *one*? So this pervasive belief prevents millions of U.S. citizens from making their way to the polls. There is a slight disconnect, however, as it is through our votes that we have the power to effect change most easily. Consider this. If all the other non-voters holding parallel positions to your own made the effort to vote, how might the outcome of many elections be different? How might our country and our *world* ultimately be different?

While we human beings tend to act in our own best interest, ignorance, in the literal sense of the word, prevents us from doing so much of the time—especially when it comes to money and politics. We avoid political discussion for fear that differing viewpoints may lead to a heated argument. Instead, we should welcome opposing points of view and be informed enough to offer our views effectively. If we engage more freely in respectful discussion, the truth might rise to the top, or at the very least we might be exposed to divergent views rather than blindly adopting those of the media. Too often, our perspectives are based on false, misguided or purposefully maligned information.

Politicians often interfere with the natural order of things, especially during a crisis. For example, after the stock market crash of 1929, the Smoot-Hawley Tariff Act was passed in June of 1930. This increased trade tariffs to historic highs and helped usher in and prolong the Great Depression. Many historians suggest that the prospect of the protectionist Smoot-Hawley legislation may have actually had a hand in the 1929 market crash. This makes sense as free trade works best for capital markets and capitalism in general. Politicians, however, feel intense pressure from special interest groups and often fail to see the forest through the trees, missing the long-term outcome from their immediate political decisions.

Throughout American history and right up to present day, there has been a temptation to protect American jobs via trade restrictions. What must be remembered is that free trade has always provided people the highest quality products at the lowest prices. Even if trade restrictions work initially, they ultimately fail because they go against our human nature of acting in our own best interest and seeking the best value at the lowest price. Free trade forces competition, always a good thing. Competition, in turn, prompts innovation, productivity and efficiency—also a good thing.

A case in point here was the Japanese competition within the global automobile industry during the 1970s. During that time, their cars were being purchased more and more by Americans for their superior quality at reasonable prices. This resulted in American car manufacturers and their trade unions clamoring Washington for legislation to protect high-paying American jobs. Ultimately, American manufacturers were forced to create better cars more efficiently to compete head-to-head with the Japanese automobile industry— good for consumers *and* the American car manufacturers.

Imagine what would have happened if back in the '70s the U.S. had set tariffs so high as to make Japanese cars prohibitively expensive for Americans. American car manufacturers would not have been forced to make better cars more efficiently. This, in turn, would have hindered their ability to compete with foreign manufacturers and export our cars around the world as they do today. The result would have been American consumers being forced to pay higher prices for an inferior product, and this probably would have touched off a trade war with Japan, one of our biggest trading partners. The transition which competition forces is initially painful but always best in the long run.

In some cases, Americans simply can't compete because of situations beyond our control in particular countries. Two current examples are India and China. Because of relatively cheap labor in these countries, the U.S. abandoned much of its manufacturing here at home. This has transformed our economy into a more service-oriented system.

It has also made Americans more productive and efficient, making better use of human resources and ushering in greater innovation with our product offerings to the world. Far more technology now takes root here in the United States. Our biotech and pharmaceutical companies, for example, are competing more successfully and often leading in the global pharmaceutical arena as well as other specialty industries. This, in turn, provides better paying jobs for Americans, resulting in a higher standard of living.

Passing protectionist or isolationist legislation is typically detrimental to a country. The Great Depression is a good example of how the ramifications of political leaders' decisions/policies can interfere with the natural equalizing effects of capitalism. Far more egregious examples can be found simply by going back to the countries throughout history that did away with personal property ownership and rights, adopting communism. As recent history has shown, communism fails because it runs contrary to the human nature of self-interest. The Soviet Union imploded economically under the weight of communism and ceased to exist as a nation. Even though a world military power, they were a third-world nation economically. The same is true for communist China. Even though the Chinese government is still communist, it is only since China embraced capitalism in recent decades that it has begun the steady climb to becoming an economic world power.

Communism may be an extreme example, but in many ways the less extreme socialist nations are finding it equally difficult to compete. This is due in part to providing a myriad of social benefits which are quite costly. These social programs have a hand in creating less productive societies in that the more a country provides for its citizens, the less its citizens do for themselves, and the less motivation citizens have to stretch and be as productive as possible.

Even though these so-called liberal philosophies have been shown not to work in many cases, idealists continue their concerted efforts to force them on the masses. Liberal philosophies sound good, and everyone enjoys getting something for nothing but as they say, "There is no free lunch." The true cost of such programs is more than simply adding up the monetary costs. The productivity loss to a nation's citizens is prohibitively expensive and unacceptably damaging.

People who are fiscally liberal believe that the government is the appropriate vehicle to take care of the masses and can do so more efficiently and fairly than the individual can. They generally believe that higher taxation renders everyone better off. They also believe the government to be the best vehicle to redistribute these taxes for the common good and accomplish this objective of everyone being better off (by way of benefit programs).

This line of thinking is flawed and inherently ineffective, however, because it goes against our human nature of self-interest. While it is true that the beneficiaries of these programs become better off initially, the vast majority of people become *less* so because of the rising tax burden required to support such programs. It can also be argued that even the beneficiaries become stripped of their innate motivation to provide for themselves. Deep down, most people understand this and that's why most fiscally liberal people have a difficult time defending their belief in higher taxes and bigger government. At the table of debate, they tend to use emotionally-charged arguments to defend their higher-tax stand, such as giving even more to the poor or the children. When societies cross a certain beneficial threshold they risk disenfranchising the working poor.

On the other hand, those who are fiscally conservative believe you should keep more of what you earn, and that government does not exist to make all things equal for all people. They feel government should exist simply to be responsible for providing what individuals *cannot* provide for themselves—such as national defense and enforcing the rule of law. They too have a tough time defending their beliefs because of the emotional arguments generated by the advocates of those who don't or can't do for themselves. After all, what caring, moral person can argue that the most helpless among us should not be provided for? Of course we need to take compassionate care of those in need. The problem here is that once programs are instituted for the truly needy, those programs are slowly liberalized, then accessed and ultimately abused by the less needy, those who are otherwise able to do for themselves.

So the attacks from each political position go on and on and our society becomes more polarized. Who is right? The answer, I believe, lies in the middle. Pure democracy by definition is "mob rule" and provides little if any protection for minority interests. This doesn't work for Americans. The same can be said for pure capitalism. There is a need for social programs within a capitalistic society to provide for those who truly cannot provide for themselves, but vigilance is also required to prevent these programs from spreading to those who would abuse them.

While idealistic and sounding good in theory, pure communism doesn't work either because conceptually, it values all people equally thereby eliminating any incentive to better oneself. Why work hard or at all if you're entitled to the basics of life regardless of what kind of effort you make? If your lot in life is fixed, where is the personal incentive to work harder? Living in this "fixed position" creates individual dependence on the state. The state, being a collective sum of the masses, is then too weak to sustain everyone when no one is producing enough to sustain themselves.

Socialism is too closely linked to communism. By trying to provide the basics to the masses in an otherwise capitalistic society, it eliminates the incentives capitalism offers through confiscatory taxation. It creates too much dependence on the state and also hinders efficiency, innovation and hard work.

Pure capitalism, while not a form of government, has its drawbacks because it often puts too much power in the hands of a few and doesn't protect or provide for the masses in any way. In a free society, however, capitalism tends to be complimentary because it's buffered through both the people's rights and the government. Other than a benevolent dictatorship—arguably, the most efficient form of government—a capitalistic, democratic republic with an agreed-upon constitution outlining rights of individuals and a rule of law is by far the best form of government. The founding fathers of these United States understood this well, and that is why, even though we represent only 4.5% of the world's population, we have grown into the richest, most powerful nation on earth. Our form of government unleashes the human spirit and provides the vehicle through which the individual and individual rights reign supreme.

To the extent that our collective views, the government and our laws move away from these ideals, the less efficient and effective the government, citizens and the country as a whole will be. The individual's right to control his own destiny, to benefit from decisions and hard work, and the unimpeded ability to better ourselves and live the life we choose is paramount in creating a free and thriving society. When we begin moving away from personal freedom and responsibility we grow dependent on others or government to supply our needs, losing personal control and motivation. Many of our individual choices then dissipate and are left in the hands of government or those running the programs we depend on.

Defining government's role in a free and capitalistic society is essential and enforcing that role while avoiding the temptations of unnecessary liberal programs, is equally essential. Government should provide for the national security and a nation's sovereignty. It should provide for those among us who truly cannot provide for themselves. It should provide, through the enforcement of the rule of law, for the protection of the health and welfare of its citizens. And finally, government should provide for the infrastructure necessary for its citizens to be as productive as they choose to be.

Anything beyond this deprives people of their God-given right to benefit from the choices they make in life. Depriving people of the benefits from their good choices or protecting them from the consequences of bad choices is as destructive as stripping them of their choices in the first place. A case in point is excessive taxation, depriving people of the benefits for making good choices while providing excessive social programs that protect people from the consequences of their irresponsible choices.

Social Security is yet another excellent case in point. In August of 1935 with the Great Depression as a backdrop, Franklin D. Roosevelt signed into law the Social Security Act. At the time, the average age of mortality was 55, so setting up a program that didn't begin until someone reached the age of 65 seemed harmless enough, thinking few would benefit from this program or come to rely on it. Who would have thought then that it would grow into one of the largest and most expensive benefit programs this country has ever had?

The program initially cost just 2% of payroll taxes, but over the years has grown to a hefty cost of 15.3% of payroll taxes, shared between the employer and employee at 7.65% each. As our citizens grew used to this government safety net, the program and its costs became more palatable, making it more acceptable for our government to expand the program. It is now the monster of benefit programs destined either to bankrupt the country or break its promise to millions of future beneficiaries who have paid into the program for 45+ years.

Unfortunately, most have relied on the program too heavily for their retirement. Knowing Social Security is there waiting, too many have subjugated their own responsibility in saving for retirement to the government. Liberalism is always tempting but sinister in its corruption of personal responsibility. We must therefore be vigilant in recognizing any form of expanded government and the politicians proposing unnecessary increased government programs, voting them down and the politicians out. In the end, the damage caused by fiscal liberalism is greater than any good it provides.

The bigger government grows and the more it does for the people, the more dependent people become on government and the less self-reliant and productive they become. We should think hard before voting in politicians who promise more government handouts. A free lunch is always tempting, but the cost down the road is far from free and less compassionate than one might think when the effects on people, including beneficiaries, are taken into consideration. As the Bible and other religious or spiritual books teach, it is far better to teach a man to fish than to provide him with a fish.

The best government can do is to offer incentives for people to do for themselves—initiatives to save for retirement, create emergency funds and anything else that offers the individual direct control and responsibility. The more successful the government is with policies promoting self-reliance, the stronger our society and our country will be in the long run. We are all better off when it is in our best interest, our self-interest, to provide for ourselves. To do otherwise has been the demise of every other democracy throughout history.

Scottish historian Alexander Fraser Tytler, born in 1747, just 29 years before the birth of the United States, summarized my thoughts throughout this chapter when he said:

> A democracy cannot exist as a permanent form of government. It can only exist until the voters discover that they can vote themselves largesse from the public treasury. From that moment on, the ma-

jority always votes for the candidates promising the most benefits from the public treasury, with the result that a democracy always collapses over loose fiscal policy, always followed by a dictatorship.

The average age of the world's greatest civilizations has been two hundred years. These nations have progressed through this sequence. From bondage to spiritual faith; from spiritual faith to great courage; from courage to liberty; from liberty to abundance; from abundance to complacency; from complacency to apathy; from apathy to dependence; and from dependence back to bondage.

While I don't see Americans in shackles at the end of a slave master's whip anytime soon, from a psychological point of view, I think this is as true now as it always has been. Dependence leads to psychological bondage, and it is human nature to repel bondage. Those who are limited in choices and completely dependent on a job often resent their bosses while those talented enough to pick up and find employment elsewhere, do not. Extrapolating, those who have relied so heavily on the state for their sustenance as to ignore the need to become self-sustaining often grow to resent the system that provides for them. This is only human nature, and human nature yearns to control its own destiny. Anything or anyone which hinders the journey of self-control is bucking human nature and bound to fail.

We witness this principle at work not only within the largesse of government but also in our family lives. As parents, we try and teach our children independence and self-reliance. If we are successful at parenting, as our children grow older and more independent, at some point they begin to buck the control we have over their lives. These can be tumultuous times as any teenager or parent can attest to. Expanding this out, there is little difference when a new territory yearning for self-control and independence breaks away from its mother nation—as when the United States declared its independence from England—a tumultuous time in history but no less based in human nature than a teenager making the natural progression from childhood into young adulthood.

It is notable that when this nation was founded, only landowners had the right to vote—those who paid taxes and had a stake in how the country was run; those who understood that the government was no more than a sum of the citizens who provided the means for the government to exist in the first place. It wasn't until the mid to late 1800s that most states changed their constitutions and allowed non-landowners the right to vote.

Today, about 50% of the American population falls into an income category that relieves them from paying any federal income tax. Knowing this makes it is easy to understand how we as a nation continue to vote in politicians based on what they promise in benefits. We give little thought to the cost of these benefits because relatively few are actually paying for them. This was the fear of the founding fathers and the foundation of Alexander Tytler's commentary above depicting the demise of democracies.

We have all heard the reference that people get the government they deserve. By voting in leaders who refuse to lead, refuse to do what is best for the nation before self, who lack the courage to do what's right and promise constituents more than the government can afford, we slowly destroy the fabric of self-reliance that made this country the greatest, most powerful nation on earth. And while people believe they are voting in a free lunch, the eventual cost is dear, both monetarily and psychologically.

From a psychological point of view, it makes us more dependent on government and less self-reliant. This saps our strength as we relinquish control over our lives piece by piece, becoming more complacent and apathetic. This should seem familiar not just from having read Alexander Tytler's quote above but because you see and feel it in everyday life. Dependence is by far the steepest price we pay because it thwarts our creativity and innovation.

But this is not the only price we pay. From a monetary point of view, the non-taxpaying masses voting in "free" benefits actually pay dearly via the stealth tax known as inflation. When a politician has neither the courage to raise taxes for social programs (in fear of alienating their taxpaying voters) nor the courage to admit we can't afford more sweeping social programs (in fear of alienating the voters looking for government handouts), then the choice comes down to this—either borrowing the money and leaving a larger debt for future generations or printing the money and diluting the monetary base, causing inflation.

This inflation impacts the lower middle class and the poor more negatively because it raises the price of goods and services they need. The lower middle class will simply pay a higher price for the box of cereal where the poor, no longer being able to afford it at all, may have to go without it entirely. It is an ironic chain of events because the people that push for more and more social programs end up paying a dearer price for those "free" benefits.

Inflation is a difficult concept to comprehend. I will therefore devote an entire chapter to inflation in Part Two of the book as it is vital to understand its role within almost every financial aspect of your life.

13

CREATIVITY IS KEY

IT MAY SEEM obvious, but in order to create opportunities, you have to start with a little imagination and creativity. You have to give some thought as to what your natural talents, interests or passions are and figure out how to benefit from exploiting them. The next logical step is to determine how others can benefit from them as well. This is what makes your talents valuable.

There are thousands of stories about how people used their creativity to spark thriving multi-billion dollar businesses and achieve wealth. Microsoft, Berkshire Hathaway and Google are but a few examples of what can be accomplished when a penchant for something you have a passion for is combined with living in a free, capitalistic society. You're limited only by your imagination. This is why so many people are willing to hang on, waiting years to immigrate to the U.S. and other free capitalistic countries. It is also the basis for my impatience with people who were blessed to have been born here but don't take advantage of this blessing.

My situation was probably similar to many successful entrepreneurs. Growing up, I developed an interest in architecture and took drafting classes in high school, moving on to obtain an architectural engineering degree in college.

Unfortunately, I graduated into the recessions of the late '70s and early '80s when there was little work for full blown architects let alone someone with an architectural engineering degree. I did manage to obtain several jobs in different types of engineering firms for a few years, but made very little money. So after being laid off from my last engineering job, I began selling real estate. I also started investing in real estate and buying what little I could afford.

I bought my first house by borrowing the down payment from my in-laws and paying them back with interest over the next two years. During an amicable divorce a few years later, I bought my ex-wife out of the property, renting it out for income while leasing an apartment for myself in a two-family home closer to work. The owner of that two-family home decided to sell the property a year later and asked me to buy it. Cajoling the bank for that loan was challenging but between two jobs, proof of rental income and letters of reference, I acquired it.

I remarried after a few years, and about a year into my second marriage, in 1984, our son was born. My wife and I then refinanced the property with a 15-year mortgage so that when our son graduated from high school we would have the means to pay for his college education either by selling the property or refinancing it. This worked out incredibly well. The refinancing was not only enough to pay for his college degree but also provided the means to buy more property.

Not only was my son born in 1984 but, feeling that real estate sales didn't coincide with family life, I also changed careers. I took a job as a financial planner with a large firm and after my formal training there I went on to acquire my CFP certificate in 1987. This left me with a broad understanding of finance, tax law and economics. I saw how the government used tax law in directing private capital to specific areas of the economy, one of those areas being real estate.

Having a penchant for architecture, it was relatively easy for me to look at a property and visualize what it *could* be rather than what it was. This helped in my real estate sales career but even more so when buying a property on my own accord. The savings and loan debacle of the late '80s and recession of the early '90s provided the perfect backdrop for several real estate opportunities. As real estate prices fell in the late '80s, banks began foreclosing on many properties and ended up owning many of these foreclosed properties. As banks went under, the FDIC took over the bank's assets and sold off the bank-owned real estate at auctions, offering financing for buyers of these properties. I bought several properties this way. After closing on a property, I used credit card debt to renovate the property enough to resell or rent it. I resold several of them for a tidy profit, which helped supplement my income and provide the funding to buy additional properties. I then refinanced those I kept and rented them at an amount high enough to pay back any credit card debt used to fund the renovations as well as enough to carry the new mortgage. This was all done part-time while working as a financial planner.

I partnered with one of my clients in 1997 in order to become more involved in real estate acquisitions. His desire was to diversify his wealth beyond his company by investing in real estate. His role was to loan the money necessary for the down payment of any property I found that would pay for itself, assuming 100% financing. Not that any bank would offer 100% financing, but my partner's down payment was structured as a second mortgage that would be paid at the same rate as the bank's first mortgage and on a monthly basis as well. In addition, I got paid a fee for managing the property. The equity in the property was then split between the two of us.

As you might imagine, locating properties to fit this criteria was not easy, but that was my role in the partnership. My time became split between my financial planning practice and this new real estate endeavor. Typically, the acquired properties needed work and were underpriced accordingly. One of our first acquisitions was indicative of what we would typically get involved in. The property was a six-unit, 100-year-old building in a decent area but in need of extensive renovations with five of the six units already rented being at least habitable.

Real estate prices had languished during the previous decade, and the gentleman selling the property was asking $205,000. Looking up the records, I found he had purchased the property less than a year earlier for only $167,000 and had not yet completed any renovations. I inquired as to why he was selling after buying so recently. He told me that the opportunities in another area of interest were much better, adding that he could pick up buildings for $10,000 per unit there if he could only act quickly. Having this advantageous information, I made him an offer to take him out of this building for $165,000 and to do so within only a month. He was happy to accept.

Once acquiring the building, I set out to make it all it could be. The empty apartment had to be the smallest two-bedroom I had ever seen. It featured a tiny galley kitchen you could barely turn around in and bedrooms more aptly labeled oversized closets. As it stood, the apartment would probably fetch about $800 per month in its current condition.

I proceeded to renovate the apartment completely, taking advantage of an expansive attic space. On the first floor, I created a large kitchen with a spacious living/dining area combination. I then added a circular stairway leading up to what used to be the attic where I added two good-sized bedrooms with incredible views of the ocean. The renovations cost about $25,000, and the apartment rented for $1,200 per month—now attracting a discerning tenant which is always the best kind.

Borrowing that $25,000 was costing me under $200 per month, and I was now bringing in an extra $400. It turned out that an existing tenant saw how beautifully the apartment turned out and moved from his existing one-bedroom into the new two-bedroom. This then provided the opportunity to renovate that one bedroom, making substantial improvements and justifying higher rent per month. I eventually renovated all but one apartment and maximized the income I was receiving for the building, thereby drastically increasing its value.

A few years passed, and I bought my partner out for $350,000, nearly doubling the value on our original investment. Six years later, I then sold the building for nearly twice that amount.

Meanwhile, we purchased a foreclosed property, a large luxurious home on Cape Cod. It was in serious need of updating as it had been 10 years since any work had been completed on the property. As it turned out, everything that could go wrong did, beginning with an attempt to get the existing occupants to leave. Between a judge trying to overstep his legal authority and a court system mishap, the previous residents didn't end up leaving the premises for four months. When they left, they had stripped everything they could possibly dismantle—every plumbing fixture, light fixture, an eight-seater indoor hot tub, a wall oven, kitchen and bathroom sinks, toilets—everything. They were prosecuted, but the case was dismissed by their claim that they believed those fixtures were theirs. Regardless, we renovated the home and sold it, making a $75,000 profit.

We then purchased an old inn with plans to renovate only to discover it was in such bad shape that it had to be torn down. What was intended to be a simple, straightforward, four or five-unit multifamily rehab project turned into a $1.8 million dollar, eleven-unit condominium complex. I eventually netted a profit of over half a million dollars but had to hold and rent the units for a few years initially until the market improved.

Another property we bought at auction for a very low price (just $115,000) was a log cabin on eight acres. The reason we acquired the property for such a low bid was because it looked like a junkyard. Adding to the ambiance, the owner being foreclosed on was standing behind the auctioneer looking like a junkyard dog in his six-foot-two, 240-pound frame, complete with plaid handkerchief around his head and missing front teeth. The image would have been complete if he'd been holding a shot gun, but he wasn't.

As it turned out, I spoke with him before anyone else arrived and he was a nice guy—but I was the only one who knew that. My concern was that the property might have been a hazardous waste dump because of the great number of junk cars, trailers and trucks on the property, but the owner assured me it was clean and valuable stuff, at least to him. After being the high bidder, I made a deal with the man. If he would get rid of all the junk and sell it, he could keep all the proceeds from its sale, and I would give him another $2,000 to boot—provided it were all gone by the time I passed papers.

And so one month later, I passed papers on a nice log cabin located on a pristine, eight-acre lot, free of any "valuable" debris. I rented the property for a few years, then subdivided off two lots to a developer for $220,000 and renovated the cabin. I continue to own it as a long-term rental that pays for itself after taking out a $200,000 mortgage.

About five years into the partnership, my partner asked to be bought out because his business was growing and he needed the money to finance that growth. One year prior to buying my partner out, however, we bought a rooming house that turned out to be an incredible deal. I responded to the tiniest three-line ad that appeared only once. As it turned out, there were two owners. One didn't want to sell and the other was desperate to sell. The asking price was $650,000. I offered $575,000 which the one partner, desperate to sell, accepted immediately. Unfortunately, the other partner wasn't budging. This is where a little creativity was needed.

Little if anything was owed on the property, so I structured a sale where the motivated partner would loan me back $200,000 of his proceeds at 0%, with $2,000 per month paid for four years with a balloon payment of the balance due after that. The savings in interest over the next four years on that portion of the purchase price made the difference between the asking price and my offer price. It also allowed me to use very little of my own money, especially beneficial with my partner no longer there to help in the process. The motivated selling partner was in essence loaning me the down payment and discounting the price by eliminating the interest on his second financing. Understanding the seller's motivation helped me put together a deal that was a win-win for all three people involved, myself and the two sellers.

After passing papers and purchasing the property, I hired a manager to live on the premises and manage the property, leaving me free to attend my growing business activities and ventures. This was the last property purchase with my partner. I proceeded to buy him out of all properties in the two years following.

The last property I bought prior to property prices escalating beyond reason, from a purchasing point of view anyway, was a combination convenient store and four-bedroom colonial, both on the same lot. I purchased the property at a foreclosure auction and should have known this property would be problematic from the get-go.

After sizing up the property at auction, I opened the bidding at $450,000—but even though there were a dozen or so other registered bidders, there were no other bids besides my own. Going once, going twice, sold. I sensed immediately that I had made a mistake. Although I had acquired the property at a good price, my opening bid had been too high. It wouldn't be the last mistake I would make on this property.

Within a week, I was contacted by the store's manager, a relative of the prior owner who had gone belly-up. He made me a proposition to reopen the store under a new name and manage it for me. I asked the obvious question, "If it didn't work before, why now?" He explained that they had attempted to support too many families, three to be exact—his own (including a wife and daughter), his youngest son's family and his brother who owned the store.

His explanation seemed to make sense. So I asked what was in it for him, and he said simply "the job of managing the store." But convenience-store managers don't make a lot of money. So this didn't ring true and should have put me on guard, but I agreed to his proposition and came up with an incentive program. This was mistake number two. In hindsight, I should have realized I was being a stereotypical male as described in Chapter 11 and done more due diligence.

Being convinced that he was competent, I reasoned that if I put together an incentive agreement, then I could motivate this person (whom I didn't know from Adam) to excel in the position. I set up the agreement that he would share 30% of the profits and receive a substantial bonus if the store made a profit by the end of any given year.

We opened in February of 2003. I lost money monthly with few exceptions. As the months went by, my manager kept giving me excuses as to why we were not making a profit—excuses which actually seemed logical at the time. So in an effort to change things up a bit and make the store succeed, I took his advice to add a deli and hire his wife to run it. Mistake number three.

Then he and his wife suggested preparing take-out food and baking our own bread. I agreed. Mistake number four.

After building a complete commercial kitchen and going to a myriad of auctions to buy kitchen and deli restaurant equipment, I continued to lose money every month. Our sales were going through the roof—but so were our expenses. So my manager suggested I hire his son (who supposedly had experience buying products at better prices) in an effort to reduce costs. I thought we would give it a try.

Mistake number five.

In order for his son to come to work for us, I was asked to put a health insurance plan in place. I did, and this was mistake number six.

Then the son convinced me to start selling lottery tickets to increase foot traffic and create another profit center. As we still didn't have a profit center yet, I agreed. Mistake number seven.

We were now in our sixth month, had a full delicatessen, selling soups and sandwiches and cold cuts, even baking our own bread. We employed half a dozen full-time employees, half a dozen part-timers, and I was *still* losing money each and every month.

Frustrated as you might suspect, I spoke with a business broker and inquired about selling. He gave me some extremely bad advice by telling me I could get a multiple of the store's sales as a selling price for the business, regardless of the expenses. Having absolutely no experience in a retail business, I believed him and seeing as how sales were continuing to go higher each month, I felt a little more secure that I could at least recoup my losses if I were to sell. That was *big* mistake number eight.

This prompted me to hang in there and hope the manager, trying to take advantage of our agreement, would turn things around.

Count this mistake number nine.

Then in November, I got a little surprise. The lottery informed me that our account had gone negative and we needed to add money to it. In my mind, this was impossible because all the lottery money was channeled into a separate lottery account, including our lottery profits. We had never taken *anything* out of this account except payment for the tickets themselves. Turns out, the manager's son had stolen over $10,000 in lottery tickets, scratching lottery tickets to support a drug habit.

He was fired. By now, tired of losing money and with no hope of the store having a profitable year, I let my manager go as well. Years later, I discovered proof that he and his wife had been robbing me blind, the very reason the store was losing money every month. Apparently, the incentives I built into our agreement to benefit them were not as much as they could steal and stealing provided instant gratification.

New plan. I cleaned house, got rid of the health insurance and hired a new manager, someone I had known for many years and could trust. Slowly but steadily, the store began losing a little less money each month until May of the second year when we actually turned a profit.

Then in early June we had a fire that destroyed the kitchen and back half of the store. Feeling encouraged by our turnaround under the new manager, I decided to rebuild which was, you guessed it... mistake number ten.

Four months later we reopened. Having to acquire all new help, the store was never the same, and the sales never rebounded to where they had been before the fire. From that point on, we never had a profitable month. I kept the store open while looking for a buyer, but one never came along. So nearly three years to the day of opening the store, I closed its doors. Three months later, I sold the building for nearly half a million dollars and finally recouped most of my losses.

In order to do this, I again had to get a little creative and condominiumize the property to separate the store from the four-bedroom colonial located on the back part of the lot. I had attempted to sell the home years earlier but needing serious renovations, it hadn't moved. So I spent $80,000 making the house like new. And this, my friends, was mistake number eleven.

I had forgotten the first three rules of real estate: 1. Location 2. Location 3. Location. Unfortunately, because the house was behind the store, it didn't sell at an appropriate price, regardless of how nice it was. Once more, using a little creativity, it eventually sold, and between the price I got for the house and the price I got for the store, I just about broke even. What I lost were three years of my life but in return, I gained a number of valuable life lessons.

First lesson. Never open a cash business unless you are going to run it yourself. The temptation for employees to steal from an absentee owner is simply too great. Although I was forewarned about this prior to opening the store, I had to learn the hard way.

Other lessons? Don't throw good money after bad. Accept when you make a mistake and move on. Cut your losses early. Identify specific goals and a time table for achieving them. Don't make the mistake of believing everyone is like you—just because you are honest, don't assume everyone else is. And just because I would have been motivated by a generous incentive program, I should not have assumed that my manager was equally entrepreneurially-minded.

The saying I bought into that drove me to get involved with the business end of the store rather than stick to the real estate end of things was a common one as well. "Nothing ventured, nothing gained." But as we discussed in Chapter 11 regarding the gender-specific traits of men and women, being the typical guy, I had jumped in without doing enough due diligence and paid a hefty price for doing so.

After purchasing this property, mortgage interest rates dropped, causing the beginning of the housing bubble. There were no more bargains to be had, and I stopped attending foreclosure auctions because retail buyers (people buying for their own use) were bidding prices beyond the intrinsic value of the properties being auctioned.

The ramifications of this bubble would not be felt until it burst in 2007 and beyond, ushering in the credit crisis and recession of 2008 to 2009. Increased foreclosures of upside-down homes (where the mortgage amount is greater than the property value) had banks buying back most foreclosed properties because there were few if any bidders willing to pay a price beyond what the bank was owed.

The lower mortgage rates, while eliminating the opportunity to buy properties at reasonable prices, offered tremendous opportunities in the refinancing of all the property I owned. This reduced the carrying costs of the properties by hundreds of dollars each month. So while one opportunity was eliminated, another made itself available.

Patience became the order of the day. I didn't buy another property until the fall of 2007 when banks started selling the properties they had bought back in recent years through foreclosure. In order to reduce property inventories, the banks sold their properties at auction at vastly reduced prices, creating another opportunity similar to the Savings and Loan debacle of nearly 20 years earlier.

Fast forwarding, during the past six years a few business partners and I have purchased over 20 additional properties. Some were sold, but most we maintain as investment properties.

Sometimes waiting patiently is necessary in order to find the right opportunities, but when opportunities don't readily present themselves, creative strategizing is in order. At this point in the economic cycle, unless the right opportunity presents itself, it could be years before I purchase another property. But if prices rise too high to offer bargain properties, then the opportunities may lie in selling a few of those properties.

Time—and patience—will tell.

14

THE AMERICAN "UNION" vs CHINA, RUSSIA, BRAZIL AND EVERY OTHER LESS-DEVELOPED NATION

CHINA, RUSSIA, INDIA and Brazil are just a representation of the developing countries of the world. They happen to be the four that may, in all likelihood, have the greatest impact on the world economy during the next few decades. How that happens will have a serious impact on the more developed nations of the world—on you and the people you know.

Out of necessity, these four countries, along with many other developing nations, have realized that only by embracing capitalism and free market policies can their economies grow and share in the wealth fostered between nations with free trade and capitalism.

As a closed-off communist country, China had remained backward and extremely poor. Its communist government had a difficult time even feeding its impoverished population. At the same time, Hong Kong, considered a part of China but under British rule until July 1, 1997, grew to be a thriving capitalistic society. Because of its favorable corporate tax rate and policies, it became home to more international company headquarters than anywhere else in the world.

This dichotomy between Hong Kong's economic success and the impoverished mainland was impossible to deny or ignore. So for many years prior to the rule of Hong Kong reverting back to

THE AMERICAN UNION VS EVERY LESS-DEVELOPED NATION

the People's Republic of China, even though contrary to communist beliefs and policies, the Chinese government used Hong Kong as a blueprint for the incredible growth in southern China and its mainland cities of Beijing and Shanghai.

The USSR had an equally bad experience employing the communist philosophy. Its economy imploded and fell under the weight and inefficiencies of a communist government and society. Years later, after shedding its satellite nations, Russia is just now in the process of rebuilding its country and economy.

While India and Brazil were never communist, their government policies prevented their respective countries from participating in the benefits which a free, capitalistic society yields. This has changed in recent years, albeit slowly, and both are now reaping the benefits with their citizens, companies and countries all better off and beginning to flourish. Positive economic change and the resulting added growth won't be a straight line up as change presents challenges, but the populations in each of these countries are now living better lifestyles, comparatively speaking, based on the living standards to which they were previously accustomed.

Therein lies my point. As these countries and other developing countries become wealthier, their workers will demand higher and higher wages—and why shouldn't they? Where is it written that a Chinese factory worker should get paid $1 per hour with no benefits when comparable American workers are earning $25 per hour plus generous benefits? And given this wage disparity, is it any wonder why so many American companies have outsourced their manufacturing to offshore locations? Within the context of a global economy, this has become a sheer necessity just to remain competitive.

In this aspect, America is like a global trade union, hence the name of this chapter. As a country, we are destined to suffer the same consequences over time as trade unions in this country have suffered during the past few generations.

So let's take a look at trade unions in this country which grew out of necessity. In the 1800s when this country was young, growing and much like less-developed nations are today, capitalists exploited the labor force. Unions were an offshoot, growing out of the discontent of workers and helping to create a better balance between industry and labor. It is worth noting that this could only take place in a free society where people have the right of assembly.

Government wasn't forcing people to work, but for the most part, was standing aside and letting the free market forces take place. Through workers' participation in a union, the union now had control of the labor force capitalists needed and could use this leverage to negotiate better terms, conditions and wages for its members. Is this proof that capitalism doesn't work? Hardly. It is simply an example of people on both sides acting in their own best interest.

Capitalists will always try to wield and retain as much power and control as possible. It is in their self-interest to do so. Workers will do the same, and if necessary, by organizing. It is in their best interest to do so, and it is a free society which allows this balancing to take place.

Capitalism, like a true democracy, needs checks and balances to thrive. If you think about it, pure democracy is mob rule. This is why the United States is a representative democratic republic and not a pure democracy. Our government was painstakingly formed by its founders to provide for the balance of powers in order to retain a free society where the individual is paramount. This freedom is what allows for the balancing between capitalism and labor without governmental intrusion.

This is not to say that government hasn't had to fine-tune our system from time to time to balance the creativity of capitalists trying to gain the advantage, an example being the passing of antitrust laws and the regulating of certain monopolies like utilities. There are other examples where government, over our country's developmental history, has created laws to allow for the balancing of capitalism and free trade. But sometimes those laws have been far too encroaching on businesses and have had the effect of offsetting the very balance they were or should be trying to preserve.

THE AMERICAN UNION VS EVERY LESS-DEVELOPED NATION

Currently, the United States or this "American Union" is trying to hang on to its higher wages and benefits as are many other developed nations like Japan, Germany and the United Kingdom. In a global economy, this becomes more and more difficult as markets open up and trade becomes freer worldwide. Companies (capitalists) can locate their plants and facilities wherever it makes the most economic sense.

A perfect example here is China. In previous years, when a closed society, companies from other nations could not locate within its borders. Then China realized that allowing foreign companies to locate there provided for the employment of its people and (relatively speaking) better or more affluent lifestyles versus the poor agrarian lifestyle the majority of Chinese people had. So even though China was allowing its labor force to be exploited at perhaps $1 per day and not sharing in the relocated company's profits, it remained a greater opportunity for its citizens than the Chinese government could offer them. The cheap labor force and lack of excessive regulation were all the encouragement manufacturing companies worldwide (not just the U.S.) needed to build their manufacturing plants in China.

Socialists from first world nations see this as the exploitation of poor people in China. The poor people in China see this as a viable opportunity, so much so that there are far more Chinese looking for work in the cities and these manufacturing areas than there are jobs. Over time, these laborers have demanded more pay and last I heard, were making more than a dollar an *hour* rather than a dollar per day. By any standards, this is a sizable increase over the past decade although still paltry pay by Western standards.

Eventually, the Chinese government may provide more civil liberties to its people, and its people may try and organize like labor unions did in this country more than a century ago, demanding more from the companies which employ them. However, even with civil liberties increasing in China, it's unlikely drastic changes will be coming anytime soon because of the massive population of unemployed all looking for the opportunities that manufacturing jobs offer the average Chinese worker.

It's been said that China would have to develop 13 more Shanghais to even begin absorbing the great number of people looking for jobs. And even if this were to happen, the world at large wouldn't be able to absorb the increased supply of manufactured goods. Currently, the world is flooded with an oversupply of goods from China. With a slowly growing but ultimately finite global demand for goods plus an almost infinite capacity, it will be a long time before most of the millions of people in China looking for a job have one.

China is also becoming a victim of its own success as manufacturing has begun moving to even lower-cost, less-developed countries such as Vietnam. This is in part why economic growth in China is in decline and has been slowing for several years now. The result will be that China, along with other less-developed nations of the world, will continue to export manufactured goods for decades to come at incredibly inexpensive prices.

In turn, this will keep a lid on manufacturing wages for years to come in the Western world. With few exceptions, manufactured goods from the developed nations of the world must compete with those produced from less-developed nations where labor is much less costly, especially as quality standards are becoming uniform regardless of where the manufacturing is being done. We see this all the time in our daily lives. When was the last time you bought a piece of clothing not manufactured in a developing nation?

Over time, the cycle will repeat itself. As developing nations become wealthier with their workforces more specialized, those countries will begin outsourcing the manufacturing requiring less-skilled workers, and those jobs will then move to less-developed nations. As mentioned above, this is happening already and will continue to occur.

Japan is an excellent case in point here. After World War II, as Japan started rebuilding its war-torn country and economy, it became the manufacturing center of the world. Growing up in the '60s and '70s, everything was labeled "made in Japan." Now Japan is one of the wealthier nations in the world and manufacturing there has moved offshore to China, Vietnam and many other less-developed nations. Japanese workers have evolved so far and are now paid so well that when shipping costs are factored in, it is less expensive for Toyota to build its cars and car parts for the American marketplace in Alabama, Kentucky, Indiana, Texas, Virginia, Mississippi, and California—employing thousands of Americans.

Without undue government intervention and intrusion this same dynamic will play itself out with labor everywhere, including developed areas like the United States, Japan and Western Europe.

The same issues exist with both union workers and non-union workers here in this country. Union workers are paid more and typically have better benefits for doing the same work that a non-union employee does. Why should this be? Do they work harder? Are union workers a more privileged class of people? Are they better trained?

A case could actually be made that quite the opposite is true. Back to our human nature. If an employee has a union protecting him with no inherent accountability on the job regardless of the quality or effort exerted, then doesn't it stand to reason that this immunity from natural consequences might lend itself to doing less? On the other hand, if the non-union worker shirks his responsibility or makes mistakes, he risks being fired. With this lack of protection, human nature would argue that the non-union worker would be far more diligent in all ways for fear of retribution or job loss.

Here in the U.S. and in many Western European nations, too often government requires certain types of work such as government-financed projects to be completed by union workers. Unfortunately, this is too often quid pro quo for political donations and support of politicians who make the laws. This causes a breakdown in the free market system and ultimately doesn't work.

For example, when a union's demands cause a company to charge more for a product or service, that product or service becomes non-competitively priced in the market place. This can result in a sizable drop in sales/profits and the company being forced to close its doors, resulting in many workers losing their jobs. A glaring example of this exists here in the U.S. in both car manufacturing and the airline industry. The unions have negotiated such lucrative wage and benefit packages for employees that these companies are either technically bankrupt or on the verge of bankruptcy.

It took the financial crisis of 2008 to push America's car companies over the edge—with General Motors being taken over by the government and Ford and Chrysler taking huge bailouts. In order to remain competitive in a global environment, these companies were forced to shed jobs. In some cases, the unions ultimately acquiesced and accepted pay cuts just to keep the respective companies solvent. A critical, pivotal point comes when having a job at a lower wage or with fewer benefits is better than having no job at all.

As described previously, this is a global occurrence. If a U.S. or Western European company has a choice between hiring workers for $1 to $2 per hour while providing no costly benefits versus paying workers $25 per hour plus benefits (costing an additional 30% of the hourly wage) where would the company be better able to produce a competitively-priced product, ultimately generating a greater profit? The answer is obvious and explains why the U.S., Western Europe, Japan and other developed nations are no longer manufacturing-based economies. These nations have become more and more service-oriented economies because it is far more difficult, if not impossible, to outsource service jobs to other countries.

Over time, the chasm between labor costs in developed nations and less-developed nations will narrow. This will be a slow, painful experience for workers in the U.S. and other developed nations as they struggle to get by on less, but a windfall for workers in less-developed nations as their wages rise respectively. It will add to the high growth rates in the world's less developed nations as they play catch-up and become a major factor in slowing the already anemic growth rates of the world's more developed nations.

Regardless of how much workers of developed nations look toward their governments to prevent this cycle, they can't stop it. As they say, it is already "baked in the cake." Politicians in developed countries can and will try adopting draconian measures in an attempt to appease their constituents, but this will be to the detriment of their respective economies, and eventually those governments will be forced to abide by the global market's demands or bankrupt themselves while trying to buck the trends.

The only hope and opportunity for the U.S. and more developed nations of the world to maintain their advantageous edge is to maintain their relatively free societies that spur and breed innovation and imagination, thus benefitting from creative solutions provided to meet worldwide needs and problems. Their respective governments must do everything possible to resist the temptation of passing draconian, protectionist laws and adopting socialistic policies that cannot, over time, be either afforded or sustained. These policies only postpone the inevitable and are extremely detrimental to the economy.

France and the other nations of Western Europe, for example, are now collapsing under the weight of their socialistic policies and being forced to take unpopular but necessary steps to eradicate the socialistic errors of the past in order to free their economies from these excessive burdens. We can't afford to make the same mistakes here in the United States, but I'm afraid it is only human nature to try and avoid the financial pain that will lead to more socialistic policies here in this country. It will take responsible leadership, courage and a serious understanding of the global economy to keep from falling behind the advancing third-world nations or adopting Western Europe's failed, socialistic policies.

15

DON'T KILL THE GOLDEN GOOSE

A SERIOUS CHANGE is desperately needed in our attitude toward taxation here in the United States. We have a progressive tax system (takes a larger percentage from high-income earners than low-income earners) along with a complicated tax code—and tremendous criticism exists of both.

Well-respected, intelligent people have recommended different solutions ranging from a flat tax (same tax rate for all, regardless of income) to a VAT (value added) tax, to a national sales tax, to the total elimination of the IRS and our complicated tax code. These arguments have been based partly on fairness, partly on the excessive administrative costs and partly on eliminating what is considered a repressive, intrusive IRS agency. Some suggested changes are also intended to capture lost taxes from the underground cash economy (cash which can't be tracked or traced). These are all well intentioned ideas.

In truth, our tax system *should* be equitable with everyone paying their fair share, but without the ever-present threat of the autonomous IRS agency swooping in and declaring automatic guilt of tax fraud prior to proving such guilt. The nation's loss in productivity from filing tax returns, audits and more is also extremely inefficient and another good argument for tax reform.

So how should we go about revamping our entire tax system? Prior to moving ahead on this, we must first consider the alternatives and look at the notion of taxation from a philosophical point of view. Then we will be able to work from a principled position anchored in human nature and self-interest.

So how can paying taxes be in our self-interest? Let me share some thoughts. The first principle to agree on is that taxation is important and necessary, and I think a strong case can be made for this. It is simply a fact that it would be impossible to do what we do as a country on an individual basis with no tax revenue. Individually, we could not defend our country, afford the institutions which maintain the rule of law and justice, provide the vast infrastructure needed, offer a public education to our children or care for the truly needy. Taxation is therefore necessary to maintain our free, capitalistic society, the "American Way" that provides our nation's ability to survive and thrive. Enough said.

If everyone pays their "fair share," couldn't it be argued that those who take better advantage of our free capitalistic society (the wealthy) should pay more than those who don't? Hence, the argument for a progressive tax system where the more you make, the higher percentage of tax you pay seems appropriate. This is the tax system currently in place and the reason the top 1% of earners pay 35% of all income tax collected (which is more than the combined bottom 90% of earners) and why close to 50% of earners pay no federal income tax at all. This seems more than fair to me, but many still feel the wealthiest among us still don't pay enough.

To that end, I would like to share the following anecdote. I don't know where I got this or who the original author is but it illustrates the point beautifully. Suppose that every day, 10 men of different income levels go out for a beer. The bill for all 10 comes to $100. If they paid their bill the way we pay our taxes, it would go something like this:

The first four men (the poorest) would pay nothing.

The fifth pays $1.

The sixth pays $3.

The seventh would pay $7.

The eighth pays $12.

The ninth pays $18.

The tenth man (the richest) would pay $59.

So that's what they did. The ten men drank in the bar every day and seemed quite happy with this arrangement, until one day, the owner threw them a curve. "Since you are all such good customers," he said, "I'm going to reduce the cost of your daily beer by $20." Drinks for the ten now cost just $80.

The group still wanted to pay their bill the way we pay our taxes so the first four men were unaffected. They would still drink for free. But what about the other six men—the paying customers? How could they divide the $20 so everyone would get his "fair share" of the windfall?

They realized that $20 divided by six is $3.33. But if they subtracted that from everybody's share, then the fifth and sixth men would each end up being paid to drink his beer. So the bar owner suggested it would be fair to reduce each man's bill by roughly the same progressive percentage amount as they paid and he proceeded to work out the amounts each should pay:

The fifth man, like the first four, now paid nothing (100% savings).

The sixth man now paid $2 instead of $3 (33% savings).

The seventh man now paid $5 instead of $7 (28% savings).

The eighth man now paid $9 instead of $12 (25% savings).

The ninth man now paid $14 instead of $18 (22% savings).

The tenth man now paid $49 instead of $59 (16% savings).

Each of the six was better off than before. And the first four continued to drink for free. Once outside the bar, however, the men began to compare their savings.

"I only got a dollar out of the $20," declared the sixth man, and pointing to the tenth man, he exclaimed, "But *he* got $10!"

"Yeah, that's right," said the fifth man. "I only saved a dollar, too. It's unfair that he got ten times more than I did!"

"That's true!" shouted the seventh man. "Why should he save $10 when I saved only $2? The wealthy get all the breaks!"

"Wait a minute," yelled the first four men in unison. "We didn't get anything at all. This system exploits the poor!"

The nine men surrounded the tenth and beat him up.

The next night, the tenth man didn't show up for drinks, so the nine sat down and had beers without him. But when it came time to pay the bill, they discovered something important. They didn't have enough money between all of them to cover even *half* of the bill!

The moral of the story? If you eliminate the most productive among us, you eliminate the country's ability to pay for, among other things, the needs of the *least* among us. A tax break by its very nature should provide greater benefit to those who pay most of the tax.

There are some notable points to be made here. First, when taxes are reduced, everyone benefits by having more spendable income. Second, when people get benefits without paying for them, a certain entitlement with a total lack of appreciation takes hold. Third, the wealthy and more well-paid expect they will pay far more in taxes and for the most part, are content in doing so.

But when you "beat up" the wealthy with over-taxation and create a class-warfare, entitlement-driven society, *everyone* suffers.

The attitude that people who earn substantial amounts of money should pay so much as to eliminate their incentive to earn is self-defeating. If you think about it logically, true wealth is seldom obtained alone. It usually takes a creative thinker or entrepreneur of sorts to come up with a business idea initially, but by employing many others, the entrepreneur makes more money than he could ever have made on his own and provides jobs as well. It only makes sense that the employees should contribute more to the company's profits (the owner's wealth) than what that employee *costs* the company. Otherwise, it makes no sense to accept the risk of running a company, putting your money on the line, and being responsible for making payroll each and every week—and, I might add, be the one to forfeit pay during lean times when making payroll would be impossible to do otherwise, as many small business owners have done on occasion.

If it weren't the case that every employee should contribute more to the company's profit than his cost to the company, then companies would make no profit. No one would ever buy stock in companies, and those companies would never grow or pay dividends. Then the wealthy would never start the company in the first place. The incentive for profit is the driving force behind all business, all investment, and what drives capitalism itself.

Without incentive for profit (capitalism) there would be no companies, no employees, no taxes collected, no government to provide protection, infrastructure, support to the needy, education for the children and the myriad of other benefits of a civilized society. We would still be a nation of hunter-gatherers roaming the plains and searching for our next meal.

The other problem with "beating up" or overtaxing the wealthy is that what they do benefits all of us. It's not only the wealthy but usually those with some means who start companies and employ the general population. If those who would otherwise start companies aren't the entrepreneurial types, then they typically buy investments (stocks and bonds) that go toward capitalizing and providing funds for businesses that provide employment to the general population. If they instead are totally risk averse, then they stick their money in the bank, which then loans the money to small businesses and individuals, also essential to a healthy economy.

After all is said and done, regardless of what the wealthy or those with means do with their money, they can't take it with them. Their money gets passed down eventually to the next generation which continues to do all the aforementioned things with it or simply spend it. If they spend it, then it benefits the companies and employees who sell whatever these beneficiaries end up buying.

If this money doesn't get passed down, it is usually because it went to charity or a foundation that continues to provide benefits to society long after the wealthy individual has died. The foundations set up by wealthy individuals and families provide much of the medical research that has made this country, and the world as a whole, a far better place. Without the money that some of these foundations funnel into charities year in and year out, those charities would not be able to help those desperately in need across the world.

Attacking the wealthy and reducing their incentive to create, work and thrive is equivalent to killing the goose that lays the golden eggs—the last thing you want to do. On the contrary, you want to fatten that goose as much as possible, getting that goose to be more productive and lay even more golden eggs, employing more people, spending more money, creating more foundations, all of which adds to our economy and betters our society as a whole.

A progressive income tax with the lowest rates possible provides for this outcome. It only stands to reason that lower rates can also increase revenues the government collects in taxes. If you can keep more of what you earn, then there is simply greater incentive to earn more.

A flat tax, on the other hand, would have the middle class paying the same rate as the wealthy and dampen their ability to get by. If the middle class is paying more in taxes, it can't afford to spend as much. When less is purchased, profits dwindle and even the wealthy who own the companies or the stock in those companies earn less.

A VAT tax or value-added tax is one that gets added to every product in each stage of its development, but ultimately all of the incremental taxation simply gets passed on to all consumers in higher prices, not just the wealthy.

And finally, the appeal of a national sales tax is that it is designed to capture the underground economy when in fact it doesn't assure this at all. On the contrary, it provides a huge incentive to do quite the opposite, to avoid the sales tax altogether. Even if it did accomplish this goal, who ends up paying the bulk of the taxes collected? The poor and the middle class. The poor and middle class spend as much as 100% of what they earn or at least a much higher percentage than the wealthy do out of necessity. This is why the wealthy can afford to save, invest and maintain their wealth, because they don't have to spend everything they make on necessities. A sales tax shifts the burden to those who can afford it the least, making everything that much more expensive and providing more incentive to avoid making purchases in the first place. This does not make for a healthy economy.

As for eliminating the IRS and the voluminous, complex tax code, making some changes are in order, but it is not a good idea to throw the baby out with the bathwater. The government does need an authority that *inspects* what the government *expects*. The government expects taxpayers to abide by the rules and pay the taxes due based on those rules (our tax code); inspecting what is expected is a basic premise ensuring all rules or laws are followed in addition to taxes being paid.

Thinking this through, if a teacher never asks to see your child's homework assignment, it will just be a matter of time before that child stops doing his homework. So while the IRS is necessary in this sense, there should never be an authority where we as citizens are assumed guilty with the onus being on us to prove our innocence. We live in a country where we are innocent until proven guilty, and the same should apply when the IRS determines an audit is necessary.

The tax code is the government's way of funneling capital into parts of the economy that need private funds and incentivizing people to fund areas of the economy that the government should not be funding or could never afford to fund. It also helps government provide tax incentives for behaviors it feels are beneficial to society as a whole.

Consider tax deductions, starting with charities. By making charitable bequests tax deductible, this provides incentive for those who can afford it to support charities they deem worthwhile. Making mortgage interest deductible provides an incentive for people to buy a home and become far more vested in their community as well as more financially stable over time. Filing jointly as a married couple provides a benefit for being married, and marriage provides for a more stable family environment which benefits society. A deduction for depreciation of an investment property provides incentive for people to invest in multifamily homes and rental properties that provide the vast majority of rental units across the country. Investing in office buildings or strip malls provides affordable space for businesses to flourish. These are but a few of the hundreds of examples in which the government uses the tax code to direct investment and provide for the betterment of society. The tax code could and should be streamlined and simplified, but to eliminate it would hurt the government's ability to steer investment into parts of the economy which need private funding.

The country's lost productivity in administering and interpreting the tax code, with the armies of accountants, tax preparers and tax attorneys, is a necessary evil. But it does have benefits as well, not only in the employment of people in this field but as a check and balance to the fairness of the tax code itself.

So while taxes across the board could and should be lower, and the tax code could and should be simpler, and the IRS could and should assume the innocence of any taxpayer in an audit, the foundation we have in our current tax system here in the United States provides the best platform to work from. If we lowered taxes and stopped the class warfare, instituted pro-growth policies favoring wealth building and making it easier for everyone to build wealth, this country would provide an even better environment for all to prosper.

To the extent we make it easier to succeed in America, fewer people need government assistance, and this savings could be redirected to programs that impact society more positively. To the extent we make it easier to succeed in America, the more attractive we are to successful immigrants which would help grow our economy. To the extent we can make it easier to succeed in America, the more worldwide capital is attracted to our existing companies and new businesses, providing additional jobs and economic growth. To the extent we make it easier to succeed in America, the wealthier our society becomes and the more revenue the government collects to more efficiently and effectively provide for infrastructure, national defense, enforcing the rule of law and assisting those truly in need.

Ultimately, making it easier for people to succeed in America is in America's best interest, and this is an attainable goal for our free, capitalistic society and our country.

16

THE SOLUTION: AMERICA'S EMBRACE

THERE IS A viable option for the otherwise inflationary solution to the problem of overwhelming debt and meeting the future obligations of the United States and most developed nations. This is to embrace policies that may seem bold and new but are actually what the American founders knew would work all along. They founded the United States on the premise that a free, capitalistic society guaranteed certain unalienable rights to its citizens and would empower the human spirit, creating a nation unsurpassed in opportunity.

The essence of this is written into the opening of the Declaration of Independence:

> We hold these Truths to be self-evident, that all Men are created equal, that they are endowed by their Creator with certain unalienable Rights, that among these are Life, Liberty, and the Pursuit of Happiness...

The document goes on to state that the powers of the government should be from the consent of the people and if government becomes obstructive to these principles then it should be abolished and a new government formed, laying its foundation once again upon these principles.

While the United States isn't perfect, I feel it is as close as it comes to perfection in the world today. If not, why would so many people wait patiently for years to immigrate here? And why do others literally risk their lives to come here illegally? Why, in such a relatively short span of history, have we as a country grown to be the most influential, powerful and richest nation with the largest economy in the world? It is because our founding fathers, at the birth of this nation, acknowledged the power of the human spirit. They knew that by creating an environment allowing personal freedoms to enable people to be all they could be, it would unlock a potential never before experienced in the world—and it has.

The combination of our democracy, our Constitution that protects civil liberties, our tolerance of others regardless of race, religion or creed, our strict rule of law and our capitalistic system of free enterprise, allows *all* citizens the opportunity to attain the American Dream. No other nation provides such a potent combination of capitalism and freedom necessary for the entrepreneurial human spirit to flourish.

There is something unique, something special about the United States of America. Embracing these fundamental principles and exploiting this country's attributes is the solution to creating the unprecedented growth needed to repay our debts and meet our future obligations. Furthermore, as we succeed, countries throughout the world would follow suit, eliminating the often necessary but unpopular aspect of our current foreign policy that at times imposes or tries to impose our views and policies on other nations. All countries would be forced to follow our lead simply to compete in this global economy.

Sounds great, but what exactly would have to be done to accomplish this, and what obstacles lie in the way?

OBSTACLE #1: CORPORATE TAX RATE

Reduce our corporate tax rate to a flat 15% or similar incentivized tax plan. There is notable and somewhat remarkable world-

THE SOLUTION: AMERICA'S EMBRACE

wide precedence for this being an extremely effective method of increasing commerce, economic growth and jobs. There is a reason why Hong Kong is the home to more international corporate headquarters than any other city on the planet—*Hong Kong's corporate tax rate is the lowest in the world.*

In the mid '90s, Ireland's economy was in shambles. They took their cue from Hong Kong and adopted a 12.5% corporate tax rate. Over the next 10 years, their economy grew faster than any other European nation as worldwide corporations flocked to Ireland to establish themselves and take advantage of the low tax rate. What Ireland achieved was a knowledge-driven, high-value, open, flexible and responsive economy. Not only did they reduce the corporate tax rate, but they also created tax agreements with many other countries, including the United States, to eliminate any double taxation on corporate earnings. They also provided tax credits for research and development as well as other incentives for international companies to establish operations in Ireland—and close to 1,000 foreign companies have done so since adopting the change in policy. The demand for employees exceeded Ireland's ability to provide the qualified workforce needed. This drove labor costs to a level where it started mitigating the low corporate tax rate benefit. The United States, with a much larger and well-educated population, would not be hindered by those same limitations.

The United States has one of the highest corporate tax rates in the world, the primary reason why so many companies are reestablishing themselves in other countries with lower tax environments. And while it's easy to criticize those big, bad corporations for acting to avoid what they feel are confiscatory tax rates here in the U.S., we as individuals do the same thing every day.

What's the difference when California pensioners move to Texas to avoid the excessive taxation in their home state of California where their high pensions were procured in the first place? Many higher tax-rate states in the Northeast are losing populations to lower tax states, many of which are in the South. The following chart illustrates where we stand as a country in comparison to a number of other countries.

CORPORATE TAX RATES

COUNTRY	%
IRELAND	12.50
CHINA	25
NETHERLANDS	25
UNITED KINGDOM	23
JAPAN	25.5
GERMANY	30
BELGIUM	33
FRANCE	33.33
USA	35

Source—Deloitte & Touche, 2014

It requires a substantial increase in corporate profits to offset the detriment of the higher corporate tax rate here in the U.S. The policy that needs to be adopted is illustrated here in principle and is not intended to provide all the details and changes the United States tax code would require to adopt such a change in policy. Simply put, a change in this direction and of substantial magnitude would provide the same results illustrated by the Ireland and Hong Kong examples.

OBSTACLE #2: IMMIGRATION POLICY

We need to revamp and expand our immigration policy. This would require providing an express program for those who could bring wealth and/or jobs with them or have the talents and professions we need. A thorough investigation would have to be completed on each immigrant to prevent importing terrorists or people

THE SOLUTION: AMERICA'S EMBRACE

hostile to our culture and way of life, and afterward, a green card offered with a fast track to citizenship for these immigrants.

Next we would have to secure our borders and deal with the population of illegal immigrants already in the country. One possible program dealing with the challenge of illegals might be a onetime "blue" card with similarities to the green card. Offer a blue card to every illegal currently in the country with a requirement that they secure health insurance, self-paid or employer-paid, and they can never be eligible for any social programs—no subsidized housing, no welfare, no food stamps, no Social Security, nothing, and never the right to vote.

By accepting this blue card, they are given the same opportunity they currently have being here illegally, but will no longer live in fear, hiding in the shadows or existing in a "shadow economy." They would be here legally and pay taxes on their income based on the tax bracket they fall into. Anyone found without a blue card or in violation of their blue card requirements would be immediately deported. Any blue-card holder convicted of a violent crime would be deported to their country of origin or jailed. This would require doubling the size of ICE (U.S. Immigration and Customs Enforcement) and other immigration agencies initially simply to implement and enforce the program. People here illegally would have three months to conform, about the same time it would take to train all the new immigration officers. At that point, we would begin deporting anyone without a blue card.

There are other details that would need to be addressed but this way, current illegal immigrants would no longer be illegal, nor would they be a burden to society. Future illegal immigrants would be prosecuted and deported immediately. Any employer found employing an illegal immigrant would face serious consequences and severe fines. Strict enforcement would be the key to ensuring the success of this new program.

Many people, most of the liberal persuasion, wouldn't like this new program, claiming it to be unfair for blue-card holders paying taxes but getting no benefits, claiming taxation without representation and a whole gamut of contrived injustices. But keep in mind here that no one would be forcing illegals to accept this blue card. They could leave and come back through the usual legal channels like all the other people waiting to come to the U.S. They could then obtain a green card, working toward citizenship and once citizens, have the right to vote and receive all benefits afforded American citizens.

One benefit afforded blue-card holders would be that employers could no longer exploit them with underpayment and no benefits. They would be legal and subject to the same employment protection laws afforded all American citizens. They would also be eligible to contribute to a 401k, saving for their own retirement, receive unemployment benefits, if eligible, and every other benefit which legal employees deserve. They would simply not be eligible for government-sponsored social programs. Either way, it would be their choice. We must acknowledge that past immigrants who helped make this country great came here looking for an opportunity, not a handout, and we therefore need to embrace the principles of personal responsibility which helped make this country great.

OBSTACLE #3: WELFARE

We would need to revamp our welfare system. Nothing destroys human innovation, initiative and incentive more than a handout. Nothing suppresses the human spirit more than the inability to provide for oneself. Conversely, nothing is more uplifting than realizing the fruition of dreams by one's own accord. The best thing our society can do for those needing help is to help them help themselves. This type of help manifests itself in college programs, retraining programs, civic job programs or others designed to give someone in need the ability to be a productive member of society and provide for themselves and their family.

I'll repeat the adage that it is far better to teach a man to fish than to give him a fish. Of course, short-term relief is in order

THE SOLUTION: AMERICA'S EMBRACE

here, but only short-term relief, and only for those willing to accept the type of self-help program or work doing anything they possibly can do. Anyone unwilling to contribute should be eliminated from receiving benefits. Unfortunately, there are those who are incapable of doing for themselves, and in this case, state and federal governments need to work together to provide for their compassionate care.

Children are a prime example of this type of need. Aid for dependent children is already available and being paid for by government, but some if not much of that aid never reaches the children in need. Too often, the parents of these kids aren't responsible enough to use the aid for the benefit of their children, using it instead for themselves or worse, squandering it on addictions. Direct aid to parents of needy children must therefore cease in order to eliminate this abuse and incentivize those parents to do for themselves. Capable adults should not be able to live on the aid meant for their children who are incapable of doing for themselves. Aid must be direct and funneled specifically to the children.

Fortunately, the infrastructure to provide for needy children is already in place within our public school systems across the country. The schools should be open early, providing breakfast before school as well as lunch, then remain open late, offering dinner to our children in need. This would allow parents of these needy children to work without worrying about the care and safety of their kids while on the job. It would also eliminate children of certain ages from going home to empty homes.

The cost of such programs would be easily afforded by the savings derived from the elimination of the abuse in the current welfare system. Food stamps, as well as most other programs, could then be eliminated. As far as housing goes, all checks for housing assistance would be paid directly to landlords if the housing wasn't already public housing. Every effort should be made to see that no public assistance money ever gets into the hands of otherwise capable adults.

Keeping these principles in mind, similar programs for seniors and the infirm could be created to provide necessary care. Society should only help those willing to help themselves or *incapable* of helping themselves. No more. No less. This would cut the costs of government assistance dramatically and reduce the number of people on assistance, encouraging a far more productive society. It would empower otherwise needy people and eliminate the victimization of those people by liberal social policies. Again, we have to embrace what made this country great, encouraging personal effort and responsibility while limiting our social responsibility to those truly in need.

OBSTACLE #4: HEALTHCARE POLICIES

The government healthcare programs of Medicare and Medicaid also need more than a little tweaking. This process is complex and complicated with much expertise needed to make valid suggestions. That being said, while not being an expert, I suggest that there are experts capable of offering meaningful suggestions for reducing waste and rendering the programs more efficient, and simply beginning the change process with a number of common-sense suggestions would save untold millions.

Tort reform should be paramount among such changes. Billions are awarded yearly to victims of medical malpractice. With attorneys reaping one third of the financial settlements, it is always in the attorneys' best interest to sue for damages whenever the slightest possibility of a settlement exists. Often the healthcare professional's counsel or insurance company will settle simply to avoid a lengthy and expensive court battle. This could be the reason why there are more attorneys in this country than engineers, and it needs to be addressed.

One possible tort reform would be to assess all legal costs to the losing side or have a jury determine how much, if not all, of the legal costs should be borne by the losing law firm and/or victim. This would eliminate frivolous lawsuits and keep avoidance settlements at a minimum. It would also drastically reduce malpractice insurance premiums which for some surgeons, cost over half a million dollars per year. These expenses are built into healthcare costs and are one of the factors driving those costs to the point of being unaffordable.

Regulations could be established to monitor and eliminate careless or incompetent doctors and healthcare providers from the system. Only the most egregious of medical malpractice cases should be litigated or settled. Even then, financial awards should be within reason and not make instant multimillionaires of victims. After all, no healthcare professional makes the decision to purposefully hurt a patient—accidents happen and are part of life. The greater good of society must be taken into consideration when reforming tort law. There should also be a limit, well under the current 33%, put on the percentage of the settlement that an attorney can charge in tort cases. This might eliminate some of the motivation on the part of attorneys to blindly pursue such cases.

One suggestion regarding the high costs of prescription drugs might be for the government to receive these drugs at cost from any company that has been the recipient of government research grants. It seems to me that if the government (taxpayer) is providing the money needed for research and development of a prescription drug, then the company receiving that grant should not be able to turn around and charge Medicare or Medicaid recipients outrageous costs for those drugs. This would save untold millions in cases where much medical research is government-sponsored.

These are but a few common-sense suggestions that could be developed into government policies and ultimately provide tremendous savings to the healthcare system without the socializing of medical care in this country. I'm certain far better, more detailed suggestions would come directly from the healthcare industry itself if the proper incentives to generate ideas were put into place.

OBSTACLE #5: SOCIAL SECURITY

Social Security needs to be turned back slowly to the safety net it was designed to be rather than the semi-retirement plan it has become. When Social Security was initially instituted in the United States, it was designed as a safety net to help those who lived well beyond the average age of 55. Therefore, only if you lived 10 years longer than the average age of mortality in America were you entitled to collect, but as our general population began living longer, the age to collect should have gone up. If it had, based on the average American's mortality of 80 years old, only those reaching age 90 would be able to collect. But as the Social Security program and its benefits expanded, the FICA (Federal Insurance Contributions Act) tax increased accordingly. With increasingly large sums coming out of every worker's paycheck, it became nearly impossible to extend the time when citizens could collect.

Social Security benefit and coverage changes took place in 2003. At that time, the full-benefit age for collecting retirement benefits began to increase gradually from age 65 to age 67. For those born in 1937 or before, the age remained at 65 with those born between 1937 and 1942 qualifying for full benefits at 65 plus some months, depending on their birth year. If born between 1943 and 1954, the age for full benefits changed to 66, and if born in 1960 or later, to age 67. Although a step in the right direction, there is still additional work to be done if this program is to remain viable and fiscally sound.

Another structural change could be an income eligibility requirement. As much as I am against paying into something that you will never collect, this would define Social Security for what it should have been—a safety net, not a retirement plan. There are many eligible Americans now collecting Social Security as their retirement entitlement who simply don't need it as a retirement safety net. The income requirement could be set high enough to ensure that if someone were denied their benefits because their income exceeded this limit, they would not endure any hardship in retirement.

If FICA taxes were looked at more like premiums for an insurance policy against possible impoverishment in one's old age, then the attitude toward Social Security would be the same as any other type of insurance. Insurance provides for the unexpected. How many of us purchase life insurance hoping to collect? We all buy insurance, often paying high premiums, in the hope of never needing it. We buy it to protect those we love in the event we are suddenly not around to care for and support them. Collecting Social Security should not be an expected part of retirement but a safety net, only available and used if necessary.

If Social Security were restructured in these ways and we adopted other cost-saving policies as well, we could reduce the FICA tax or keep Social Security from facing bankruptcy in the future and possibly both. For those who desperately need and depend on Social Security, the program needs to be preserved, but the more we can reduce costs and enable and encourage workers to save and be responsible for their own retirement, the better off all of us will be moving forward.

CHALLENGE #1: TRANSFORMING PUBLIC EDUCATION

Revamping our public education system is an absolute must. Getting a good public education should continue to be an entitlement for all in this country, as it is one which benefits society as a whole and is very much worth the burden of costs involved. But as the quality of public education deteriorates throughout the country and with costs spiraling out of control, the benefit to society is dwindling and in some cases, nonexistent.

The main reason for this is a lack of competition and the elimination of market forces inherent to every other part of our society. If you are in a department store and see two sweaters at the same price, you will always select the one you deem higher in quality. If you seek quotes for work where quality and standards are specified, then the lowest price always wins out.

This same competition should be present in the public education system, but unfortunately, the exact opposite is true. When a school system isn't providing an adequate education, the solution always seems to be funneling more money into that school district. Based on this constant, it could be said that there is an incentive for schools to underperform in order to receive additional funding. In most cases, it is not the funding that is lacking but rather how those funds are allocated, often being mismanaged. The lack of quality teachers and administrators is also a fundamental part of this equation.

In many cases, the teacher unions are at fault by instituting programs like tenure which places serious restrictions on firing educators, making it nearly impossible to remove teachers who deserve to be let go. Nowhere in the private sector does anything like tenure exist, nor should it. If an executive working for a private-sector company for 25 years or more stops performing to the company's standards, he loses that job. The same should go for teachers. When there is no longer an incentive (remaining employed) to maintain high standards on the job, some will no longer perform to the best of their ability. Human nature is always at play in everything we do, and incentives, in whatever form, encourage people to strive harder and do their best. Eliminate incentives and for many, you eliminate excellence.

This is why the best way to fix the public education system in the United States is through some sort of voucher system where educational funding is still provided by the government but directed by the end user. The government should only become involved in the choices parents have for their children's education if and when the parents don't. If a voucher system were instituted across the nation, schools would strive for excellence to attract those vouchers. To do so, behavioral standards would have to be imposed on students in order to create the environment necessary for higher learning, and students would have to conform in order to participate in the better schools. There would then be a marked improvement in the quality of public education in this country. We should not continue spending more and more public funds while getting less and less for the money.

THE SOLUTION: AMERICA'S EMBRACE

Students suffer by not receiving the education they need to compete for the most basic of jobs, and society as a whole suffers when this occurs and untold billions of dollars are wasted in the process. Educational decline has become epidemic in this country mainly because of the stranglehold from teachers' unions on the system. Meanwhile, politicians have grown beholden to these unions and therefore lack the integrity and courage to fix this very broken system.

CHALLENGE #2: LOWERING COLLEGE COSTS

College affordability needs to be addressed as well. Typically, I would be advocating that the current outrageous cost of a college education should be handled by the market in that the higher costs rise, the fewer students will be able to afford them, and colleges will then be forced to drop their prices in order to compete for those fewer students.

In this day and age, however, a college education is almost a requirement to have a chance at a successful future. The inability to afford a college education hurts America's youth, leaving them unequipped to compete for jobs of the future, hence jeopardizing the future of the country itself.

I would suggest here that the government use tax policy to entice private colleges to reduce their tuition, room and board and associated fees. Currently, the cost to attend a private college is twice that of state or public colleges, and sometimes more. By eliminating the tax-exempt status of any college charging more than a 50% premium over that of state colleges, it would entice them to bring their costs more in line with public colleges that are currently oversubscribed because of the huge differential in costs between the two. Then we should add an excise tax on any private college tuition exceeding 100% of what public colleges charge. This would reduce the temptation for private colleges simply to increase their costs high enough to offset the taxes due because they were no longer tax exempt.

Because of the large endowments of many private colleges (Harvard, for example, boasts endowments in excess of $32 billion), the loss of their tax-exempt status on the earnings from those endowments alone would probably be enough to have them comply with the tuition reductions. For colleges and universities that didn't comply and then paid the tax, the government could use those taxes collected to increase the number and amount of grants awarded to deserving students, build more state colleges and universities and lower state school tuition costs.

This may seem like arm-twisting and government meddling into private enterprise, but I feel quite the contrary. Every other free market enterprise pays taxes on its earnings. Why should colleges and universities receive the benefit of tax-exempt status when they charge tuition rates well beyond what is needed to provide an excellent education? These outrageous cost escalations have far outstripped those of inflation, are hurting middle class families and ultimately hurting the ability of the United States to compete with other nations, many of which provide free secondary educations to their citizens. At the same time, to ease the burden of college costs, the government should make all costs tax-deductible to those with incomes under a certain threshold. This would have to be done in conjunction with the policy outlined above. Otherwise, it would simply give rise to even higher college costs as colleges would be quick to capitalize on the fact that tuition would be slightly more affordable because of their tax-deductible status.

The obstacles and challenges discussed here are certainly not exhaustive but do offer a step in the right direction. If these suggestions for growth and government policies are enacted, helping us to overcome obstacles and meet economic challenges, then we can create an environment to provide the growth needed to offset this country's huge debt. By exploiting our advantages as a country, unleashing capitalism, and restructuring and minimizing inefficient social programs and policies, we will not only grow our way out of debt but also better provide for the infrastructure, national defense,

THE SOLUTION: AMERICA'S EMBRACE

maintenance of law and order, public education and care for the truly needy.

The larger benefit, however, would be the promotion of peace, American-style freedoms and democracy around the world. Imagine the monetary savings to all countries if there were no longer any military conflicts around the world—monumental.

And consider this. If America could embrace and accomplish these goals, our country would be attracting international corporations along with the jobs those companies provide. Imagine an America that allowed for the immigration of the best and the brightest from across the globe—then imagine the companies, inventions, opportunities, research and development that would spawn as a result.

Imagine an America that could afford to provide a safety net to every citizen without creating a government-dependent society, but one which promotes instead individual responsibility and freedom—a country with the most affordable and best healthcare in the world—one which constantly implements new medical technologies and discoveries, making that healthcare system more efficient and accessible to all citizens.

Imagine an America that encouraged and promoted individual retirement accounts and also provided income for those who, for whatever reason, could not provide for themselves during retirement.

Imagine an America where *every single child* received the proper nutrition from three balanced meals per day along with an excellent education, where secondary schooling was affordable for all citizens and tax-deductible to most. This would provide our American youth the ability to compete in the ever-expanding global economy and to secure a bright future for their families and the country as a whole.

Finally, imagine a *world* which, in order to compete with this new growing United States of America, adopted similar policies and provided the freedoms already enjoyed by our citizens to *all* people, a world where America acted as an example of how things *could* be and *should* be—an America whose policies of freedom and liberty were never imposed militarily but were freely adopted by other countries who felt pressured only by their desire to compete economically.

Imagine countries around the world pursuing prosperity through peaceful means in the best interest of their citizens and the world as a whole. If people are allotted the freedom to pursue self-interest, keep more of their hard-earned money, advance themselves financially and have the dignity that self-responsibility promotes, then the world—while never being perfect—would be a far better place.

It is simply human nature to pursue self-interest and exercise control over our own destinies. When governments create constitutions, laws and policies which provide the freedoms coinciding with these innate human desires, then those societies can't help but flourish.

Conversely, governments and regimes which dictate behaviors running contrary to these innate human desires, ultimately fail. For it is these unalienable rights endowed by our creator—life, liberty and the pursuit of happiness—for which the collective human spirit will forever strive and thrive.

PART TWO
THE BASICS

INTRODUCTION

Every topic has basics to tackle which are essential in building to a higher understanding. The same goes for money—what people do for and with money and why. So we first have to develop a clear understanding of what money *is*. Let me explain.

The obvious explanation is that money is this paper stuff that represents the value you work for and use to buy what you need or want. If this is your understanding of money, you are reading the right book. Unfortunately, here in the United States and throughout the world, this is where the understanding of money ends. This is also the reason why most people do nothing more than work for money most of their adult lives. You need to understand far more than this to be financially successful and have money work for *you* instead.

Another basic is that you must believe you *deserve* success. This goes for financial success as well as all other aspects of a successful life. Ponder this a bit, but in the meantime, let's move on.

A third basic to our understanding is that money is just a means to an end, a tool to be used. Because it is only used by humans, its flow to and from one person to another is based very much on human nature. So understanding human nature is an integral part of understanding how money works, why different investments go up and down, what explains people's buying patterns and much, much more. Included here are perceptions and marketing which help determine monetary value and how much or how little someone is willing to pay for something.

A good example of this is an old master's painting sold at auction. What makes an old piece of art sell for over $18 million, the sale price of the *Canaletto* painting? Many factors contribute to such a hefty price—its rarity, the buyer's taste, desire, how many others with means are competing for it, and/or the prestige of owning it. The primary influence on the sale price, however, is the great number of people in the world today with much more money than they will ever be able to spend in one lifetime. This factor, when combined with human nature, causes perceptions of value to become exaggerated and even skewed.

Objectively, this painting is simply an old piece of canvas with some paint on it presenting a pleasing picture by a talented master who might have taken a month or two to complete the work. So what makes a few months of one person's time (along with the cost of paint, canvas and frame) worth almost a ton of gold, the equivalent of 60 average homes in the U.S. or the collective lifetime incomes of a few thousand Chinese workers—or summing it up, enough to feed 25,000 children in an impoverished nation for a year? Only an abundance of money and our pleasure-seeking human nature can produce this subjective perception of value.

Part Two of this book will deal with the more technical aspects of this largely, non-technical book. I hate getting bogged down in the details of basic investing, but in this case it is necessary in order for you to understand where the world's money is invested and how these investments work.

So here goes. Just the facts please...

The three primary investments are bonds, stocks and real estate. Now don't jump all over me for leaving out every other investment like gold, oil, jewelry, coins or famous paintings. These three are simply the most common and basic investments and therefore the topics of the following few chapters. Before we begin, please note that bonds get broken down into two camps—bonds and cash equivalents—which I'll discuss in the next chapter.

17

CASH AND BONDS

THIS ISN'T THAT complicated. You see, a bond is a promise. Someone loans someone else money and that someone else "promises" to pay it back with interest. Looking back, I believe bonds got their start in prehistoric times as perhaps other investments did.

Let's assume Rocky the caveman spent a week meticulously sharpening a small spearhead and attaching it to a long straight stick. Dino, another caveman, walks over and asks Rocky if he could borrow the newly-created weapon to go kill something and feed his family. Rocky thinks, "Hey, I just spent all week putting this spear together." Rightfully, he asks Dino, "What's in it for me?" Being a reasonable guy, Dino agrees to give Rocky a pound of the meat from his hunt when he returns at the end of the day in addition to returning Rocky's spear. Fair enough. A bond is created.

Understanding is in the details. So let's break this down into financial terms. Rocky provides the money (represented here by the spear) which is the something of value. The spear represents a week's salary to Rocky because it took him a week of work to create it. Dino realizes that killing an animal with Rocky's spear will work more effectively than throwing rocks at it—and Dino has neither the expertise nor a week's time to create a spear of his own.

So Dino asks to borrow Rocky's weekly "salary," the spear. Rocky wants a benefit, however, for loaning his hard-earned-spear "money." In turn, Dino agrees to give Rocky a pound of meat and promises to return the spear at the end of the day. The pound of meat represents the interest (or return) on Rocky's spear investment in Dino's hunting venture—a loan of sorts to Dino. This becomes a mutually beneficial business deal. Rocky feeds his family that night on the interest (pound of meat) without having to hunt. Dino hunts more efficiently and kills more animals within the same amount of time. This makes the agreement beneficial to Dino, even after paying Rocky the pound of meat he owes him. All good.

Now all bonds, like all loans, have terms. In our prehistoric example, the term of the bond is one pound of meat (interest) to be paid at the end of the day (maturity or due date).

Two points. When Dino returns the spear, it isn't quite as sharp as it was originally—I guess some of Dino's throws ended up in the dirt. So the spear is not worth as much upon its return because it was not as sharp. This is an example of depreciation. Also, because repayment takes place over a period of time, when a bond is repaid later, the money from that bond no longer has the same purchasing power. This is an example of inflation.

In modern times, there are many examples of similar "bonds" or what could be described as bond-like investments. Start with a simple savings account. You put your money into a savings account at your local bank. By doing so, you are loaning the bank your money. A savings account is a type of "demand" account that simply means you can return to the bank and demand your money at any time—any time the bank is open for business, that is. So the term of the loan is "upon demand." The promise here is being made by the bank in that it agrees to return your money upon demand and also pay you interest at the stated rate during the period they use that money.

Getting your money back with interest is guaranteed by the bank, and all deposits of $250,000 or less are further guaranteed by the United States government, assuming it's a U.S. chartered bank. This investment, I think you'll agree, is quite safe. Hence, there is little if any risk taken by putting your money into the savings account. Because there is little to no risk of losing any of your principal (money you put in your account), this is considered "cash" or a cash equivalent. Think of it simply as another place other than your pocket to keep your cash, the only difference being the small amount of interest the bank pays you.

The bank then adds your money to its larger pool of cash. This is essentially where the money comes from when the bank makes personal loans as well as loans for cars, businesses, homes and credit cards. The bank makes its money by charging higher rates of interest to the people they loan the money to than they pay you on your account.

Here's where risk enters into the formula. The bank is taking on risk loaning your money to other people because some of those people won't pay the money back, defaulting on their loans. The bank, to keep from going out of business, has to be very careful when offering a loan. They must make sure the people they loan the money to are capable of keeping their promise to pay it back.

As a result, the bank assesses the risk of each loan on an individual basis and determines the interest rate accordingly. The higher-risk loans are paid back at a higher rate. Consequently, even if some of the higher-risk loans don't get paid back, the greater interest the bank is collecting overall on loans that *do* get paid back will more than compensate for the defaults.

Now let's consider different types of loans. Personal loans and credit card loans are considered a bank's higher-risk loans because they are only backed by a person's "promise" to pay. Collateral loans, on the other hand, are less risky because the bank has not only the promise of the individual but also attaches the item (or collateral) the loan is used to purchase—like a car, home or business. If someone defaults on a car loan, the bank then has the right to repossess (take back) the car, sell it and use the proceeds from the subsequent sale of the car to repay the loan.

For this reason, the bank would typically charge less interest for a car loan than a personal loan—the car loan is less of a financial risk. But this can get complicated because people are all different and banks ultimately need to make a judgment call in each case. Some people are more capable and live up to their promise to pay the money back better than others. This is where credit ratings come into play. As people take out loans and pay them back, the history of them doing so provides banks an idea of what to expect in the future from its customers. If someone takes out a loan, makes the payments on time and pays the loan back as promised, they create a good credit history and are apt to receive a good credit rating. So a bank is more inclined to give someone with a good credit rating a more favorable (lower) interest rate on a personal loan than someone with a low credit rating might receive on a car loan or collateralized loan.

Is this making sense? If not, simply bring it down to a personal level. Let's say you have $1,000 in the bank, earning 1%. An older family member with a good job who has a long history of paying his debts (and in whom you trust) asks to borrow that $1,000. Admittedly, there is some risk here, certainly more risk than loaning the money to the bank which is what you are doing when you put the money in your savings account. Your family member could lose his job or for some reason unbeknownst to you at the time be incapable of repaying your loan. Neither of these risks is inherent with the bank where your $1,000 currently resides. So as a result, because of the greater lending risk, maybe you charge your family member a bit more, say 2%. In this case, you now make twice as much interest for taking on an acceptable risk.

Now let's say you run into an old classmate. In catching up, he shares with you that he's had a hard time keeping a job and has been living with his grandmother because he can't afford an apartment... and he *really* needs a car. He found an old car that seems to be okay,

CASH AND BONDS

and he needs $1,000 to buy it. Let's assume he's willing to pay 20% to borrow your cash—ten times what you were going to charge your responsible family member at only 2%. In all likelihood, you probably wouldn't loan him the $1,000 regardless of the rate of interest he was willing to pay even if you had the old car as collateral for the loan. Why? The same reason a bank would not loan him the money—the risk of not getting the principal back outweighs the potential reward of making ten times the interest.

Banks and lending institutions (or the people behind them) make these decisions and judgments every day about people borrowing money. It is therefore imperative that they consider the risks involved, making certain that if they *do* agree to approve the loan, they are properly compensated via the interest rate charged for that risk—and there is always a risk, regardless of how credit-worthy the borrower might be.

So we've covered what cash or cash equivalents are—demand accounts that have virtually no risk of losing principal and consist primarily of money held in the bank. We have also covered that when you put money into a bank account, you are actually loaning that money to the bank. We delved into a bit about risk and reward and how banks make money by borrowing money from you and loaning it out to others at higher rates of interest. We also addressed the risk the bank accepts in doing so, as well as how you and your money are completely insulated from any risks the bank takes because of their guarantee as well as the government's guarantee for accounts $250,000 or less (FDIC insured).

What we haven't covered is exactly what bonds are. As stated earlier, bonds are secured by the promise to pay the bondholder back—like an IOU. Let's say you borrow $20 from a friend and to keep from forgetting it, you wrote down "IOU $20," signing your note and giving it to your friend to hold. In this example, you are the bond issuer and your friend is the bond holder. Your word and signature are your promise to pay the $20 back, but the IOU is only as good as your promise and ability to pay it back.

Most bonds are issued by the U.S. federal or state governments, government agencies, foreign governments, municipalities and corporations. The bonds are guaranteed by the issuer and only as good as the issuer's promise and ability to pay it back. Therefore, risk is involved as previously discussed because, regardless of the credit worthiness of the borrower, something unexpected could ultimately go wrong.

When risk is entered into the equation, things become more complicated. For example, how can the average person purchasing a bond assess the risk of his money being paid back along with interest? To assist the average person and institution investing in bonds in risk assessment, we have companies called rating services. These companies rate the bonds or debt and assign the bond a rating, starting with AAA (Triple A), then AA all the way down to a C rating where default is more likely. This addresses default risk or the ability and likelihood of the issuing entity to meet the terms of the bond and pay the interest and principal when it is due.

In the case of bonds, there is an even greater risk which is more difficult to assess because there is no rating service that does it for you. This is called "interest rate risk." I'll try and simplify this as best I can. Bonds are bought and sold (traded) at different prices above or below "par." Par is when a bond sells for its face value. For example, a $10,000 bond is sold for just that—$10,000—but this is seldom the case. Most often bonds are sold at a premium (more than this face value) or at a discount (less than face value). Whether a bond sells at a premium or a discount depends on the interest rate of the bond and the current interest rates, which fluctuate daily for a bond with the same terms.

Let's say you buy a U.S. government bond for $10,000. The "terms" of the bond say that the government will pay you your $10,000 back in 20 years and also pay you 5% interest yearly. So assuming the government keeps its promise, you can expect $500 per year for a total of $10,000 over the 20-year period. At the end of 20 years, the government will pay you $10,000 back. With me?

CASH AND BONDS

Now here's the tricky part. Over that 20-year period, the value of the bond fluctuates, going up and down depending on the *current* rate of interest for 20-year bonds at any given time. If you should want to sell that bond at any time prior to its maturity, you would be subject to selling it at the *current* price. This is what causes the risk or possibility for loss but also provides an opportunity for reward or gain.

Let's say two years after buying the bond referenced above, the interest rate on new 20-year bonds has fallen to 2.5%. Let's look and see the effect this would have on the bond you own. The promises remain the same in the bond you bought. It is still paying you $500 per year (5% on the money you invested) and the U.S. government is still repaying your principal (the entire $10,000) in 18 years. So nothing has changed there except that the new 20-year bonds are only paying 2.5%. Someone might rather buy your bond paying 5% instead of a new bond paying 2.5%. This someone would have to invest $20,000 at 2.5% to make the same $500 that your $10,000 bond is already paying (2.5% of $20,000 = $500). So it would make sense that this someone might be willing to pay you close to $20,000 for the bond you bought two years ago because the return ($500) would be the same. Please keep in mind this is an over-simplification for illustrative purposes only. If you sold your bond for the $20,000 offered, you would have made 5% each year and then doubled your money for a 100% gain when you sold your bond just two years later. This illustrates that when interest rates go down, the value of bonds goes up.

Unfortunately, this works both ways. Let's say in that same two years following your bond purchase, rates go up to 10%, meaning that new bonds being issued are paying $1,000 per year. Your bond is stuck with the same promise of two years ago, paying only $500 per year.

Consider the possibility of selling your bond and trying to find someone to buy it. You can understand some reluctance to buy this bond from you at the old interest rate guarantee of 5% when the new interest rate is 10%. Someone looking to buy a bond would only have to invest $5,000 at 10% to get the same $500 that your two-year-old bond is paying (10% of $5,000 = $500). Should you want to sell it, it is reasonable that someone might offer you $5,000 for your bond. So you would have made 5% each year—but then lost 50% of your initial investment of $10,000.

Did the U.S. government default on your bond? No, but you still lost quite a bit because of interest rate risk. This illustrates how the value of bonds goes down when rates go up. Even though default risk is low to non-existent in our example (being issued by the U.S. government), substantial risk remains and is something you have no control over because you cannot know at the time of bond purchase what rates will be years later.

Unfortunately, this is not the end of the risk in holding or buying bonds. The final risk is inflation unless it is a foreign bond in which case it has currency risk as well. Inflation is also a risk that is difficult to assess. It's the risk of fluctuating purchasing power when the invested money, your principal, is paid back. Let's say that $10,000 would buy a new motorcycle when you initially invested it, but 20 years later that same motorcycle costs $20,000. In this case it would be fair to say that your investment lost half its value when that $10,000 buys only half as much at the time of the bond's maturity.

So it only makes sense to deduce that inflation is not good for bonds. When inflation occurs, people are less inclined to purchase bonds, and those who already *own* bonds might want to sell. If there are more people wanting to sell than people wanting to buy, the laws of supply and demand drive the price of bonds down until the price gets low enough to entice those willing to buy. This makes bond prices drop which in turn causes interest rates to rise.

This again makes perfect sense. If inflation is running high during the term of the bond then when you receive your investment back at time of the bond's maturity, that money will buy less—so you're likely to demand a higher interest rate be paid by the bond each year or it simply wouldn't be worth your while to make the in-

CASH AND BONDS

vestment. The reward or interest paid should at least offset the risk or erosion of purchasing power caused by inflation.

To recap, there are three risks involved when purchasing a bond or loaning an entity (bond issuer) your money:

1. default risk—the ability and probability of the issuer to keep its promise as outlined in the bond agreement

2. interest-rate risk—how interest rates going up and down affect the value of your bond

3. inflation risk—what the principal will buy at the maturity of the bond when you get your money back

The lesson here is that all bonds are unique and all risk is relative...*all risk is relative*—not just with investing but in life as well.

18

STOCKS

THE EASIEST WAY to understand what you own when you purchase a stock is by comparing it to being a silent partner in a company. For the most part, you have no say in how the company is run or why it does what it does. You simply like what it does, how it does it, the profits it makes, or some other facet of the company and hence, that's why you buy the stock.

Most people purchase stock in the hope that the value will increase and they can eventually sell it at a higher price, making a profit. When you buy stock in a company, it is an equity investment. You are actually buying a little piece of the company, not loaning the company money. As a result, you receive an equivalent little piece of what the company does or earns. If the company pays a dividend that is or should be a declared portion of their profits, you will get your equivalent share. That is another way you can make money with stocks. Selling stock is one of the two ways that companies have to raise money. The other way is to borrow money from a bank or lending entity or borrow it by issuing corporate bonds and selling them to investors.

I believe the idea of stock in a company also has its roots in prehistoric times. But before there was stock there had to be someone with an entrepreneurial spirit, motivation, and an idea.

STOCKS

Let's go back to our prehistoric example of Rocky and Dino but add a few more characters to the mix.

Wilma and Jocko were a young couple living in a small cave on the edge of the village. Jocko was rather lazy and only liked to play sports or watch others play sports all day, which did not make him a very good provider. This caused the family to go hungry all too often. For wife Wilma, hunger and being married to a lazy couch potato were both good motivators. So with the motivation in the pit of her stomach, Wilma got an idea. She watched the exchange between Rocky and Dino and took note. Rocky was good at making spears but didn't like hunting. Dino, on the other hand, didn't mind hunting but was too lazy or not talented enough to make his own spear.

That's when Wilma got hit with the entrepreneurial spirit. She went to Rocky and arranged to purchase a new spear, offering him five pounds or a week's worth of meat. It was all of Wilma's savings and a good deal for Rocky who would much rather make spears than hunt. For a week's worth of work, the time it took for Rocky to make a spear, he got one week's worth of meat. This came at a good time for Rocky, too. When Dino went hunting, he had killed enough meat to do without Rocky's spear for a while—so Rocky was getting hungry.

Now Wilma had a spear, but she didn't have the strength or expertise to use it herself, and Jocko was completely hopeless, only interested in playing cave ball with his buddies. Wilma went to Dino's cave and showed him the new spear, offering to loan it to him for a day in exchange for only half a pound of meat instead of the full pound that Rocky had charged him. Dino willingly agreed, and the next time Dino went hunting, he borrowed Wilma's spear and paid Wilma the half pound of meat.

But Wilma ran into the same problem Rocky faced. Dino only needed the spear once a week. A half pound of meat, while better than nothing, was not enough, which gave Wilma even greater motivation. She found more rock-throwing hunters and showed them her spear, explaining how much more productive they could be using a spear than throwing stones. She kept marketing her spear until she found a new "customer" every day. This gave her three and half pounds of meat each week (half a pound per day x 7). Word began to spread, and soon rock-throwing hunters began showing up at Wilma's cave asking to borrow the spear, offering more than a half pound of meat to coax her into loaning it to them. Profits began to rise.

With this new motivation and growing entrepreneurial spirit, Wilma went back to Rocky who by now had made two more spears but was very hungry. She offered him four pounds of meat for a spear, 20% less than the previous price.

Rocky thought long and hard. Having lost his only customer to Wilma, he looked at the two spears just sitting there, unused. He still had no desire to hunt for himself, preferring to make spears instead, so he gave in to his growling stomach (always serious motivation) and sold another one of the spears to Wilma. He justified this by realizing that, having made a few spears now, it didn't take him quite as long to make each one, so he was still being paid adequately for his time.

Wilma then acquired seven new customers. Before long, she needed more spears which Rocky was more than happy to continue providing so he could keep eating without having to hunt. At this point, there were two businesses in the village, Wilma's spear-renting business and Rocky's spear-making business. Wilma was now paying Rocky only three pounds of meat for a spear and charging customers one pound a day to use them. Business was humming along. Hunters could still kill a week's worth of meat using a spear rather than their antiquated rocks, so everything was copasetic. Wilma put Jocko to work leasing out the spears, threatening to throw him out of the cave if he didn't contribute and now spent her days getting pedicures.

Then one day some of Wilma's customers stopped borrowing spears. Wilma looked into the problem and found they had bought their spears directly from Rocky. She immediately realized this would be the downfall of her business. She reasoned that her spears were getting dull which may have prompted the customers to buy their own.

Something had to be done and done quickly if Wilma wanted to avoid returning to lousy toenails and hunger pangs. So she hastened her way to Rocky and made him an offer to work for *her*—an offer he couldn't refuse—five pounds of meat per week with paid holidays and two weeks' vacation. Rocky acquiesced without hesitation—of course, the dull spear to his throat might have increased Rocky's motivation to accept her offer. He began creating more spears but also offered spear-sharpening maintenance on Wilma's stock of spears—making for happy customers all the way around.

However, having come so close to financial disaster with the potential loss of her business, Wilma was thinking ahead and did not stop there. Realizing there were a number of past customers who had a higher intellect than the average caveman and the innovation to buy their own spears, Wilma hunted them down, offering each a position with the "firm" as outside salespeople and opening up new villages for spear rentals. Realizing a lot of travel would be involved, she offered them a good base salary (enough for them to feed their families) as well as a percentage of profit from their sales. So the young and energetic Java and Coco became Wilma's employees. With the motivational offer of this profit percentage, they kicked it into high gear, bringing in more and more spear rentals.

Wilma soon needed more spears than Rocky could possibly make and additional spear-making materials, more than could be found in the village. She began hiring and training more spear makers and importing the necessary raw materials from other villages. These new spear makers could not all fit into Rocky's cave, so she was also looking into building a new spear-making cave, and this was going to be expensive. She could borrow the money, but then the principal and interest payments would eat into cash flow...uh, I mean meat flow.

So she decided to sell tiny percentages of her business, calling these tiny percentages "stock," short for her stock of spears. The first investors were many of the women in the villages who saw Wilma as a successful entrepreneur, in control of her own company, with employees in villages all over the land. She adorned herself with the finest furs, drove her own wooly mammoth and, of course, had great nails. Who wouldn't want a piece of that action?

Wilma quickly raised all the money needed through the selling of these stocks which she then used to build the first ever spear factory, set up spear-leasing outlets all over the known world and hired employees manning thriving rental huts in outlying villages. Wilma's company was now acquiring so much meat that she could afford to send every stockholder a half pound of meat each week. This made the stock in Wilma's company increase in value as more and more people wanted to buy additional stock so they could get their meat without having to hunt for it.

Herein lies the concept of this book: invest in income-producing or appreciating assets so your money begins working for you and you can work less for it. If cave people can do it, anyone can, and in our example, not only did Wilma become wealthy, but the people who bought her stock also acquired wealth—wealth being defined as not having to hunt (work) for every morsel of food (thing) you need, metaphorically speaking.

So stocks are ownership in a corporation, allowing investors the rights to a portion of corporate profits. If the corporation chooses to reinvest those profits back into the company, then presumably, profits would be even greater in the future, making the shares of stock more valuable even if the profits weren't distributed. Assuming there is a market for the stock, you can sell your shares for the higher value to someone willing to buy them. This is how you receive a return on your investment or the "gain" as it is called—capital gain to be precise—because it is a gain on capital you invested.

Unfortunately, stocks do not always increase in value, and every company is not as transparent or easy to understand as Wilma's

STOCKS

company. Sometimes, it is difficult to see how companies make their money. Then again, some companies do not always make money, and in fact, often lose money. These are the risks you accept when owning stock. For example, just because company profits are not paid out and are reinvested in the company, does not mean future profits will increase.

What if those profits were used to research and develop a new product line that, in the end, proved unviable? And even if the reinvested profits *do* make the company inherently more valuable, the investor will never realize that value or gain unless someone else feels the same way and is willing to bid on and buy the stock for that higher perceived value. Then you could also have mismanagement, or the market for the products the company makes could change, become less profitable or just became obsolete, driving the company out of business and making your little share of it worthless. Yes, your little share or multiple shares of stock carry all the same risks as owning your own business.

Stocks are subject to two primary risks,: business risk (bankruptcy) and market risk. To illustrate these two risks quickly, in Wilma's case, let's assume that someone discovered gunpowder and guns back in our prehistoric world, and people no longer wanted nor had the need to lease spears. There would then be no need for spears, Rocky, the factory, leasing huts, Java and Coco or even Wilma for that matter. They would all be out of work and the company out of business. Therein lies the business risk.

As for the stockholders, the following scenario probably would not develop overnight but would slowly play itself out. Initially, when reports of guns surfaced, some savvy stockholders would surely see the future hieroglyphics on the wall and try to sell their Wilma-company stock. There might likely be some people around who felt hunters would continue using spears, and those people would still be willing to buy the Wilma stock, only at a lower price.

This illustrates market risk. When fewer people are interested in buying than selling, the price of stock drops to a level where some people determine it may be a good value. But if spears became obsolete, no one would be willing to pay for the Wilma stock, regardless of price, making that stock worthless. This is market risk at its worst—no market for stock at any price.

Note that this can actually happen without underlying companies becoming worthless. An example of this was in the stock market crash of 1929 which ushered in the Great Depression. Companies did not become totally worthless, but no one was willing to step up and buy stock for fear the price would continue to drop. And the same thing happened to a lesser degree in the market crash of '87. Stocks had dropped so much that people feared buying, even at the lower prices, so markets for many stocks simply did not open, making it impossible to sell stock at any price.

This points to the difference between marketable and liquid. Many people mistakenly assume stocks are liquid, meaning they can be sold at any moment (liquidated) for cash. But only money in the bank is truly liquid. Everything else is merely marketable, with some assets being more marketable than others.

Bonds are considered safer, and their price doesn't typically change as radically as stocks. The market demand for them is much greater than for stocks, so they are more *easily* sold if needed in a crisis.

Exchanges like the NYSE (New York Stock Exchange), NASDAQ (National Association of Securities Dealers Automated Quotations) and others provide a larger market for stock, making it easier to sell than real estate, especially during a time of crisis when transactions need to happen quickly. Private stock—stock in a non-public company that does not trade on an exchange and has no set market—can be extremely unmarketable and is considered even more illiquid than real estate. All of these factors should be taken into account when purchasing stock.

19

REAL ESTATE

THIS BRINGS US to real estate, the last of the three most common investments. Whether we own or rent, we all depend on some form of real estate because everyone needs a place to live. This makes real estate unique and gives it certain advantages over other investments, but it is a misunderstood investment as well.

Many homeowners think of their home as an investment and in one very real way, it is. It is an investment that protects you to a certain degree against inflation. As the cost of housing increases, so does the value of the home you own. I am sure you have heard people say, "I could not afford to buy the home I live in if I had to buy it today," referring to how much homes in general have appreciated since they bought theirs.

The rising price of a home is a reflection of supply and demand as well as inflation. The intrinsic value of a house goes up as prices for lumber, wiring, shingles, plumbing and everything else it takes to build a house rise, including labor costs.

The intrinsic value of a home does not change much from location to location other than labor costs. For example, it costs about the same to build a house in Boston as it does in Atlanta, except for the difference in labor. The cost of housing in the Boston area is much higher, however, and this is related to supply and demand. Many factors affect the supply and demand portions of the formula such as how strong the economy is in the area and what the average salary is. Salaries tend to be higher in the Boston area, and people can therefore afford to pay more for housing—but because laborers and people in the trades are subject to those higher prices, they have to charge more for their labor, making building a house in Boston more costly than say Atlanta.

The amount of available land for expanding development also plays a part in the supply side of the pricing formula. The more plentiful the land, the lower the cost of surrounding real estate. A buildable house lot in a crowded suburb of Boston may cost twice or even three times as much as a comparable lot in a Chicago suburb, making the cost of housing more expensive. How close the property is to jobs and places people travel regularly (shopping, hospitals, public transportation, major highways, recreation and entertainment) is also a contributing factor. In addition, how safe the general area is can play a key role in the purchase price of real estate for most people.

It needs to be said, however, that all of this starts getting fairly subjective in a hurry because tastes and desires vary so greatly from one person to another. One person might enjoy living in the hustle and bustle of a thriving city within close proximity to many amenities while another prefers the peace and quiet of a rural area and does not mind traveling farther to buy what he needs. This is why you've heard it said that "all real estate is local."

What makes your home an investment are its amenities—amenities that you can do without at some time in the future. For example, if a couple needs a four-bedroom, 2 ½ bath home in a suburb with good schools for their three children and within close proximity to a city for easier commuting to their jobs, they may pay around $450,000.

Ignoring the effects of inflation at this point, let us now fast-forward to when those children are grown and the couple is retired. The parents no longer need to be near the city or in a suburb with good schools. Nor do they require a home with four bedrooms and 2 ½ baths. Instead, a smaller home farther from the city and costing only $200,000 might suit their needs. In this case, it's easy to see that the portion of their home turning out to be an investment was the $250,000—money they can now put toward other living expenses.

Add inflation, and in 25 years the house they bought for $450,000 may be worth $900,000, but the smaller house they are going to buy might be worth $400,000, making the investment portion of their house the $500,000 difference. However, it might not buy more in current goods and services than the $250,000 would buy in the first example which ignored inflation.

Even though the $500,000 does not buy any more current goods and services, it has kept up with inflation and does not necessarily buy less. This is key because it is not the dollar amount that is important in the future, but the *purchasing* power of those dollars. Imagine how much less of a lifestyle the retired couple could afford if they had not owned the house but had rented all those years, building nothing in equity. Notice also that it was only the difference between the values of the houses that was available for use for retirement income by the retired couple.

If the couple had decided they could live in a tent, they would have had $900,000 in pocket for retirement income. If they had purchased a smaller house but in a more desirable resort-type area costing the same as their larger home, they would have zero investment value or money to use for retirement.

As you can see, the needs of the retired couple are very much the determinant factor as to how much their existing home becomes an investment for retirement purposes. I may be stating the merely obvious here, but in fact, few people think this through. They just live on, watching the value of their home increase and assuming that value will be available for retirement when needed. As you can see from the example above, however, this is only true if they choose to live in a tent, and there's not much of a chance in that happening.

So much for the home you live in. How about investment or income property? The way to look at income property is to view it as a quasi-business. Anyone who has owned income-producing property knows this is true because many times it's a very real part-time and, depending how much you own and how little help you have, a full-time job or business.

The business in this case is keeping the property occupied and rent flowing in. Think of your tenant the same way a business owner thinks of an employee. A business owner doesn't hire an employee unless he will benefit financially from that employee's labor. So it is in the business owner's best interest to keep his employees happy because this is the only way he continues making money.

In a similar respect, it is in the landlord's best interest to keep his tenants happy. When tenants are content, they are more likely to pay the rent, and the landlord continues making money. Happy employees, more often than not, equate to a profitable business, and happy tenants typically equate to a profitable income property.

I say "typically" because no matter how happy the employees are, if the business isn't viable, it is not apt to be profitable or will fail entirely. The same goes for an income property. No matter how happy the tenants are, if the property doesn't maintain a healthy cash flow, then it is unlikely to be a profitable property.

What do I mean by cash flow? When the landlord/owner takes in more from the rent than goes out in property expenses, this is said to be a positive cash flow—a good thing. This is exactly what banks want to see before they consider giving you a loan to buy an income property.

Let me use the first non-owner-occupied, true investment property I bought as an example to illustrate all the risks and rewards of purchasing income property. My first income property was a six-family apartment house in a quiet, residential community. When I bought the building, it was in rough shape, empty and condemned. But it was in a desirable area, so I knew that if I could fix the place up, good tenants would likely rent the units. It was a triple-decker with two units on each floor made up of three one-bedroom apartments and three two-bedroom apartments. The only reason I could buy it at the time was because it was owned by the FDIC which guarantees all bank deposits up to $250,000 and takes over bank assets of banks that fail. The FDIC was selling the properties they owned, offering a favorable 95% financing to entice buyers to purchase them.

A little bit of history might help here. In the late '80s when the first real estate bubble burst, many banks had offered risky real estate loans that ended up being defaulted on by the borrowers. When this type of situation occurs, the bank forecloses on the borrower, and if no one bids a high enough price at the foreclosure auction—usually enough to pay the existing mortgage balance as well as the bank's costs to foreclose—then the bank bids what they are owed, ends up being the high bidder and acquires the property. This was happening all too often, ushering in the savings and loan crisis of the late '80s and early '90s, causing many banks to go under and be taken over by the federal government because the bank's deposits were guaranteed by the FDIC.

At that point, the FDIC had a non-performing asset in this empty, condemned six-unit building, one that it did not want to renovate and manage. So there was no risk for the FDIC to offer me a 95% mortgage on the property regardless of what type of property it was or the condition it was in. If I defaulted on the mortgage they gave me, the worst case for the FDIC would be to foreclose on that mortgage in which case they would end up with my 5% down payment and take the property back. Whatever payments I had made before defaulting on my new mortgage, they would keep as well—a no-lose proposition for them.

On my part, however, there was significant risk. I was out $5,000 and making payments on a non-performing asset in its current state. My only funding source at the time was credit cards…and we all know the rates credit card companies charge.

So time was a critical factor. Someone had begun restoring the building years before but must have run out of money in the middle of the project. The first two floors were intact, but the entire building needed to be rewired, and much of it needed new plumbing. The third floor was a different story. The one-bedroom on this top floor was a mess and needed a new kitchen; the two-bedroom on that floor had fire damage, serious enough to require gutting the entire apartment down to studs and rebuilding it.

I focused on rehabbing the bottom four apartments first as they required the least amount of work. Within a matter of a few months, I had the first four apartments ready and rented them out. Then I started on the top two apartments. Within five months of having bought the building, I finished all renovations, and the building was full with rent-paying tenants.

I now owed $100,000 in credit card debt but had a performing asset that a bank was willing to look at. So I refinanced the property with a $220,000 mortgage and paid off the $95,000 FDIC mortgage as well as the $100,000 in credit card debt—putting $25,000 in my pocket and owning a six-unit apartment building that was cash-flowing, meaning the rents were covering the mortgage payment, expenses and then some. All good.

I then used the money I made from that deal to buy another property at auction. This time it was a single-family building needing only a little cosmetic work. I put it on the market and sold it two months after purchase, making another $25,000. Next I bought a five-family needing little work. As tenants moved out, I went in and renovated the apartments, making them as nice as I could and raising the rent accordingly.

This brings up my two principles in purchasing and owning income property. I won't buy anything located in an area I would not live in myself, and it is much better to rent an apartment in pristine condition than to do as little as you can get away with in making the apartment habitable.

REAL ESTATE

My reasons are twofold. If you buy property in depressed areas, you will end up with tenants who can only afford to live in depressed areas, and those are the most marginal of tenants. These tenants seldom have any money in reserve and as life's problems arise—cars breaking down, unexpected medical bills or a myriad of other issues—it is often the rent which goes unpaid. At that point, regardless of whether or not you have had a good relationship with the tenant, you become their adversary.

Meanwhile, you need their rent money to pay your mortgage and other expenses—but the tenant can't pay and still needs a roof over his head. You become the big, bad perceived-to-be greedy landlord who can't relate to their dire situation and is coldly evicting them. A tenant will never understand that *you* might be living paycheck to paycheck and need every rent paid in order to cover your own obligations—how most landlords start out, and the risks are many.

Another unique real estate investment presented itself after I had created a partnership with a friend and client. This was the real estate partnership and great opportunity for both of us previously outlined in Chapter 2. As I was looking for real estate opportunities for our partnership, I came across an extremely old building that was once an inn and more recently, a restaurant. It was located within a prime residential area in a small town on Cape Cod. The lot was not zoned for business, but because the property was licensed to be a restaurant prior to the zoning, it was grandfathered in. Although considered non-conforming in its current residential zone, because of the grandfathering in of the property, it could remain this way. This, along with its recent history, provided an incredible opportunity.

It turned out that the property had changed hands a few times with its current business being a restaurant which happened to be a loud, Mexican establishment known for cheap food and stiff drinks. It attracted a young crowd—and a young crowd partying on vacation to boot.

As I mentioned, the location was in a prime, quiet, residential area. As you can imagine, the restaurant's neighbors were beside themselves in annoyance from the level of noise and the late-night shenanigans of the patrons. Adding to this neighborhood angst, the police were called regularly to either break up a fight or remove inebriated patrons from nearby properties in ground pools. The restaurant was also being run on a shoestring and finally went bankrupt.

Prior to this bankruptcy, the property had been on the market, and I had made an offer rejected by the owner. With no better offers, the property was eventually foreclosed on, and I ultimately bought it at a foreclosure auction for $40,000 less than my original offer.

My intention for the property was to renovate it into a multifamily dwelling and rent out the units. I met with the town officials prior to bidding at the auction and was assured that, even though it was not zoned as a multifamily residence, because it was non-conforming currently, it could remain that way provided a variance was approved by the governing boards. I was given the impression that with the recent history of the property, anything residential in nature along with relinquishing the restaurant license would be welcomed. That turned out to be precisely the case and a variance was issued by the town.

Having obtained all proper permits, I had just started gutting the property when the fun began. The building inspector determined that because of its age, the building could never be brought up to the current codes. This resulted in a mandate for me to raze the building—which I proceeded to do. Within hours, I was served a "cease and desist" order from the town's historical society in charge of preserving antique buildings. Having been constructed in the late 1700s, this building certainly qualified.

An internal battle followed between town agencies which I then turned into a unique opportunity. I agreed to raze the building and rebuild, replicating the architecture of the original building if a permit and variance to build eleven condo units in its place was granted. In analyzing the costs of constructing a building in Greek Revival style architecture, I determined that I would need that number of units to make the project viable. This compromise satisfied both sides, and the neighbors were even more pleased with the concept of condo ownership over rental units.

The variance and permit were granted, and over time the project was a huge success. I say "over time" because we went 50% over budget in building it. The framing alone was so intricate that we could not get a framer to even quote the job. We ended up having to frame it without a quote in which case the framing contractor charged us based on time and materials. Ouch.

Another reason for the overruns was the timing. We broke ground in February of 1999 and finished in July of 2000. Meanwhile, because of the burgeoning stock market in '99, many millions of dollars were coming out of Wall Street and the stock market and pouring into the building of mansions located off the coast of Cape Cod on Nantucket. At the time, money was no object, and the cost for contractors was soaring—which drove our costs up. When we went to sell the condos, the market had all but dried up because of the stock market bubble popping in 2000, sending the U.S. into the recession of 2001 and 2002. We ended up having to rent the condos before the market bounced back (starting in 2003) which turned out to be the beginning of the real estate bubble that has since popped. It took time, but the project eventually turned out well, with my selling the last unit sometime in 2006.

And speaking of time, it has been said that time heals all wounds. Well, time also benefits most debtors and with real estate owners being some of the bigger debtors (next to the federal government), this is a key point. It's in the federal government's best interest for inflation to exist in moderate amounts. There are two reasons for this. It keeps the economy moving and it lessens the national debt burden. By having a manageable amount of inflation in the system at all times, people continue buying goods as soon as they need them rather than waiting for them to drop in price. If you need a new car because your vehicle is beginning to have problems and new cars are getting more expensive all the time, you will buy that car as soon as possible to keep from paying even more in the future.

The opposite is also true. If the price of cars is coming down, you will hold off buying a new car indefinitely, waiting for the price to drop lower and lower. The more people hold off buying, the fewer goods are sold in the economy with spending grinding to a halt. This becomes a deflationary spiral that all governments try to avoid at all costs.

This happened in the '90s and into this century in Japan, and the Japanese economy has still not recovered completely. After Japan's stock market crashed in late '89, the Japanese people lost so much money that they stopped buying everything except living essentials. This caused the economy to go into depression with real estate prices tumbling, making the situation even worse. The Japanese government did everything possible to turn this around including lowering lending rates to ¼ of 1% in an attempt to spur demand, but it's human nature to wait if prices are beginning to come down, regardless of how inexpensive or easy it is to borrow money.

So for 25 years or so the economy of Japan has crawled along. More recently, the Japanese government has taken drastic steps in an attempt to spur the economy and inflation, but the jury is still out on whether these steps will be successful as inflation and interest rates in Japan remain among the lowest in the world.

I make a point of this because it is inflation, even at moderate levels, that offers an advantage to the real estate investor. Inflation causes the brick, mortar and lumber with which real estate is built to go up in price, thereby making it more expensive to replicate existing real estate—which drives the cost of all real estate up. Inflation also drives salaries up which allows for the affordability of higher rent as well as higher mortgage payments.

At the same time, most owner-occupied real estate loans and multi-families of four units or less have a fixed rate for long periods of time—15, 20, 25 or 30 years. So inflation alone increases the value of the property and a landlord's income, making it easier to pay the debt because his payments don't rise along with everything else, and he's able to pay the mortgage back with less expensive dollars. It never hurts to have your interests aligned with the government's interests. The government can control or influence much more than you or me and is apt to do so whenever needed as they have been since the financial meltdown of 2008 to 2009.

Anyone who has bought a house understands and appreciates the effect inflation has on real estate. When you first buy a home, it is often difficult to pay the monthly mortgage, as homes are a high percentage of your available income. Over time, however, several raises or maybe a promotion or two later, you start making more money, and the mortgage payment isn't quite so difficult to pay. Inflation is what causes this. So the next time you complain about prices increasing, think about the benefit you might be appreciating without realizing it—no pun intended. I'll cover inflation in greater depth in its own chapter because it is so integral to our current financial system.

Another principle I endorse in rental property ownership is to always rent something I'd be proud to live in myself. If you would be proud to live there then odds are your tenant will be too. This makes it easier psychologically for the tenant to keep paying the rent and caring for the property, which is also in your (the landlord's) best interest.

This also makes good financial sense. I'll illustrate this point with another six-family property purchase. When I bought the property, five of the six apartments were rented. The sixth would have rented for about $600 per month in its current condition. Instead, I borrowed $25,000 and renovated the apartment, costing me an additional $300 per month in financing costs at the time. I then rented the apartment for $1,100 per month. The additional $500 per month paid the additional financing cost and gave me an extra $200 net income. But the greater benefit was that I now had a beautiful apartment which attracted a higher caliber tenant and increased the value of the property beyond the $25,000 spent because income properties are valued mostly as a percentage of the income they create.

Another key principle in owning investment real estate is appreciating good tenants in the same way an employer appreciates good employees. I bend over backwards to make my tenants happy because they are paying down my mortgages and over time, building my wealth. Investment real estate is probably the easiest way for many people to start building wealth if their opportunities are limited otherwise. As complicated some feel real estate is, the average person still has a basic inherent understanding of a real estate investment.

There are other ways to own real estate in addition to direct ownership and personal management, but most of the same benefits exist in all real estate investments.

20

STUFF!
WHAT DETERMINES ITS VALUE

DID YOU EVER wonder why an apple might be selling for 10 cents at an orchard but the same apple selling for 95 cents at the supermarket or $1.50 at a convenience store? Same apple but many different values, and as long as they are selling, worth every penny to the one buying. Convenience plays a big part in the value of our apple—but what about other stuff?

What determines the value of anything is very simple—supply and demand. The complicated part here is what actually determines supply and demand and how those factors are impacted by different situations.

We might as well start with real estate seeing as how that is where we left off. What determines the value of real estate? The definition of value in real estate or anything else for that matter is what a buyer is willing to pay and what a seller is willing to sell for—it's all in the "willing." Unfortunately, that doesn't help us much in trying to value a piece of real estate, but it does give us a start. If we could locate a similar property sold in a similar location within the past few months, that would give us a good idea what the property we are trying to value might be worth.

But no two properties are exactly the same, and economic or social conditions may have changed since the prior sale. For example, what if a few murders took place in that specific part of town in recent months? That social condition would probably have an adverse impact on the value of property in that area. Unfortunately, changing social conditions are difficult to quantify for valuation purposes.

So instead, let's assume interest rates jumped higher in the past month or two. This would directly impact the affordability of a mortgage most people use to buy property. If the financing is going to cost more, then all else being equal, the price of property would have to come down to offset the higher interest rates.

To illustrate, assume a property sold for $300,000 a few months back when mortgage interest rates were 4%. With 20% down and a 30-year mortgage, the principal and interest payment would be $1,145.80. If rates increased to 5% during the past three months, then a comparative property in a similar location selling for the same $300,000 would cost the buyer $1,288.37 (with 20% down on a 30-year mortgage).

Now it is unlikely that someone would be willing to pay $1,288.37 per month for the same property that only cost $1,145.80 per month just three months earlier. In this scenario, even though the seller wouldn't like it much, he would have to sell the property for $273,442 for the buyer's monthly payment to remain the same as it were just three months earlier. In other words, putting $60,000 down and taking out a 30-year mortgage for the balance of the purchase price, the monthly cost would be the same whether you paid $300,000 and got a 4% mortgage or paid $273,442 and got a 5% mortgage. In both cases, the payment would be $1,145.80. Therefore, if you were a seller and rates jumped higher when you decided to sell, your property would in all likelihood be worth less than an identical property was worth just a few short months ago in the above example.

This is why real estate prices tend to go up when interest rates go down and vice versa. But this is not always the case because it depends on why interest rates are moving. If, for example, rates are coming down because the economy is weakening with people losing their jobs and fewer people able to afford a house, then even if mortgage rates are falling, this most likely won't cause real estate prices to rise. In this case, the demand for houses would have dropped, possibly causing prices of housing to fall right along with interest rates, depending on the severity of the economic downturn.

Starts getting complicated, doesn't it? So to value a piece of property, you first have to find a similar property that sold in the very recent past, subtract or add value for different features and then take economic conditions into account. The tricky part comes when this property isn't a home you are going to live in but an investment property—one you plan to resell or keep and rent. Now you not only have to find a similar property that sold recently, adding or subtracting value for different features and factoring in economic conditions, but you must also factor in future economic conditions, making an educated guess. If the economy is weakening, then your opportunities to resell or rent the property you are about to buy might be fewer, making the purchase far riskier, and you may therefore not be willing to pay the same price or even buy the property at all. All of this has to be taken into account when buying a piece of property.

The value of stuff, from property to automobiles to furniture and clothing, is subject to many of the same conditions. When the economy is strong, employment steady and jobs paying well (because companies have to pay well to attract and keep good employees), department stores don't need to generate many if any sales to move their merchandise. People simply have money and are therefore willing to pay the higher prices.

When the economy is weak with fewer people having jobs and less money to go around, stores have to compete for those fewer available dollars and drop their prices. Because of economic conditions, the store's inventory, whether it be clothing or home goods, varies up or down. It doesn't matter what the store paid for the merchandise. They can only sell their merchandise for what someone is willing to pay for it if they are going to sell it at all.

Let's follow a piece of merchandise from its origin and then back again, seeing how economic factors come into play. Take a cell phone assembled in Japan and sold in the U.S. Assume the parts cost $18 and the labor costs $12 with the cost of shipping it to the U.S. at $3. The Japanese company's profit is $8. The store in the U.S., looking for a 20% markup, prices the phone at $49.99. That would be a gross profit for the retailer of $8.99. After paying for overhead and business expenses, the store's net profit comes to $4. If they sell all of the phones they order, then they will likely order more and life goes on. The store makes enough to afford the rent, utilities, employees' salaries and benefit costs. Those employees then have money to spend in other stores and to pay their rent and living expenses. The economy is strong and life is grand.

Over in Japan, the same goes for the employees of the company who assembled the phones and the same for the companies in China, India and Germany who engineered, manufactured and sold parts to the Japanese company which assembled it. The same goes for the employees of the companies in Australia, Russia or Malaysia who sold the raw materials used to make the parts. They call this the "trickle-down theory." This also illustrates the benefits of a global economy and capitalism at work.

Say they don't sell the phones and have to drop the price to $39.99 just to move them off the shelf. Not only is the store going to lose money, but it may also have to lay off employees and possibly cut back on benefits to the remaining employees. Then when the store goes to reorder, they must tell the supplier they won't pay $41 per phone—they will only pay $31—or they won't be reordering any more phones. The Japanese assembly company wanting to stay in business lays off part of its workforce and reduces some of their remaining employees' benefits but also calls the part suppliers and reduces the price they will pay for their parts.

The part suppliers do the same, calling the raw material suppliers and demanding a reduced price for the raw materials. Those companies, in turn, do the same with their employees and suppliers. Because the U.S. consumer isn't willing to pay $49.99 for the phone, people all over the world are laid off and/or work for less. They therefore can't afford to spend as much in their respective economies, and those economies suffer, weakening as a result.

So the demand for the phone wasn't great enough to support the price, forcing the value and cost of the phone down. This is how stuff is valued. In a perfect world, everyone involved in creating the phone would simply figure out what it cost them for their contribution, from the raw materials to the retail sale, then add a profit margin and pass it on. But if the consumer doesn't find the benefit of the phone worth the price, then the value of every stage of the process is reduced. This is what happens when supply is greater than demand.

On the other hand, if the phones were in high demand and flying off the shelves at $49.99, the store would be reordering frequently. Then everyone involved in the production of the phone would have the ability to raise prices and force the retailer to ask a higher price from the consumer, and as long as the demand stayed greater than the supply, a higher price would be paid. This is inflationary and typical of a strong global economy. If more people have the money to afford stuff then there is going to be a higher demand for stuff, and everyone will be able to charge a little bit more for the stuff they produce in the process.

Then there is rare stuff. That's when the supply is very limited and demand varies based on many things, including economic conditions, marketing, personal preference and psychology. Art falls into this category. So do luxury cars, yachts and jewelry.

What makes a car worth $250,000 to $300,000 or more? What makes some paint on an old canvass worth millions? If economic conditions are good, at least for super-wealthy customers who buy rare items, and these items are marketed as one of a kind (which many items in this category are), then customers are simply paying for their *desire* to own that particular item. Driving an automobile that is unique or one few others can afford makes the owner feel special, spoiled and pampered—and this is something we all enjoy.

The same goes for wearing an exquisite piece of fine jewelry, sailing on a magnificent yacht or admiring an incredible painting hanging on your wall. Psychologically, it makes us feel good to experience creature comforts. For many of us, this desire is satisfied by simpler means, but then everything is relative as we discussed in Chapter 9.

Money in an account only has meaning when we consider what it can buy. After all, we can't eat money, and it can't clothe or house us—it's only good for what it can purchase. If you have $1,000 in your account, you can afford to buy more than someone with only $100 but not as much as someone with $100,000 or $100,000,000. It is no different for someone with a $100,000,000 net worth to buy a painting for $1,000,000 than it is for someone with a $100,000 net worth to buy a painting for $1,000. Everything is relative here. Both may be extravagant but worth it to the buyer because of the psychological pleasure he will derive from the painting. This is how stuff is valued and why the exact same stuff can vary greatly in value depending on the type of customer and economic conditions affecting that customer.

21

INFLATION:
THE CONSTANT VARIABLE

ASK ANYONE WHAT they think about inflation and they will tell you it's a terrible thing. It erodes your purchasing power and reduces your standard of living. When left unchecked, it can and often does topple governments.

Definition of inflation: an increase in the monetary supply resulting in a continuous rise in the price of goods and services. Plain English translation? The government printing bills or digital cash "out of thin air" resulting in more currency than there is corresponding growth in the economy.

It is appropriate and even necessary for the government to increase the supply of money as the economy grows. If it doesn't, both people and businesses would be vying for relatively fewer and fewer dollars. If the amount of dollars in circulation is held constant, this causes a deflationary environment which is not conducive to economic growth. Say there are only one million dollars changing hands in our fictitious economy. If the economy doubles in size over a number of years with more people and businesses competing for that same million floating around, people and businesses have to provide more and more goods or services to compete for this limited supply of dollars. As a result, as the economy grows and these dollars become more and more dear, relatively speaking, prices drop constantly. With prices constantly dropping, people put off buying in hopes of even lower prices, thwarting economic growth.

If, however, the money supply increases at the same rate as the economy grows, then theoretically, prices would stay the same as the amount of currency changing hands grows to meet the needs of a larger economy. The money supply would be held constant as a ratio or as it relates to the size of the economy. In our fictitious example, if the economy doubles, then the money supply would increase to two million and therefore the value of dollars in circulation would remain constant.

On the other hand, if government creates money disproportionate to the growth rate of the economy, then there is more money chasing fewer goods and services, and prices rise. This is inflationary and drives down the value of each dollar in circulation. If the money supply doubles to two million dollars without any growth in the economy, then the value of each dollar would theoretically only be worth half as much and prices would double accordingly. If this were to happen, you would probably demand twice your current salary because your money would suddenly buy only half as much. The business you worked for would be charging twice as much for its goods or services and therefore able to afford paying you twice as much, relatively speaking, though everything would remain the same. Even though your income doubles, it would still only buy the same amount of goods or services as before. This is inflation in its purest sense. However, because prices are constantly rising in this scenario, people are more apt to buy as soon as they need an item for fear it will cost even more in the future. This is why moderate inflation is typically good for economic growth and why governments and central banks of the world strive for moderate inflation in their respective economies.

When considering financial decisions—whether it be investing, saving, borrowing or spending—inflation should always be a consideration because it is built into our American DNA. We not only accept inflation but actually expect it. Honestly, do you ever believe goods or services will be less expensive over time? Sometimes prices go down for a short period of time but no one really expects them to go down, stay down and keep trending lower.

Is this a good thing? You tell me. Wouldn't it be better if prices were stable? If prices always stayed the same then your standard of living would increase over time as the income from your job with annual raises afforded you more and more goods and services, right?

There's only one problem with this scenario. If the company you work for never raises the price of the goods or services it provides, if their revenue/income is stable or stagnant, how can they afford your annual raise? Will you be happy never receiving an increase in pay? And if you think about it, why *should* you get a raise? If you are doing the same thing year in and year out, why should it cost the company more for this same work every year? But can you imagine you or the average worker going without a raise for five to ten years? And can you imagine any union in America agreeing to no wage increases for its members over any lengthy period of time even if all other prices were staying the same? Of course not.

Psychologically, we all want to feel our work is more valuable each year even if it isn't, and we all want to make a little bit more each year even if this increase in pay won't buy any more than your lower income bought the preceding year. This is what I meant when I said that inflation is built into our DNA as Americans. We simply expect to pay more for the same thing in the future as much as we expect to make more for doing the same thing year after year.

Reconsider the question, "Is this a good thing?" An argument can be made that it's not only a good thing but actually necessary for a growing economy. Theoretically speaking, the more money changing hands, the more the economy grows. The more the economy grows, the more jobs are created. The more jobs available, the more opportunities people have to earn more money that can be spent into the economy. The better the economy, the better the lifestyles of most people. All the while, the more money changing hands, the more income tax our government collects, resulting in more government money available to spend into the economy on defense, infrastructure, social programs and services.

If people knew the price of an item was not going to increase in the future, there would be less impetus to buy now, and many would hold off making purchases. Worse yet, if deflation were the norm with prices continually dropping, everyone would put off buying until they were absolutely desperate for a particular good or service. However, in a *moderately* inflationary environment, knowing that waiting will likely result in higher prices in the future makes the incentive to buy in the present compelling.

Simply put, the economy moves much slower with fewer dollars changing hands in a deflationary environment. Japan experienced this for well over two decades when starting in 1990, it fell into a deep recession where people simply stopped buying anything they didn't absolutely need. Prices dropped lower and lower, competing for fewer and fewer yen being spent and continued on with people putting off their purchases knowing a better deal was in the waiting. All the while, the Japanese government was collecting less in tax revenues because with commerce dropping, there was less currency changing hands.

So an argument could certainly be made that modest, controlled inflation is good for the economy. Over time, however, even modest inflation has an erosive effect on currency and savings. At a modest inflationary rate of 2.5%, a dollar will buy half as much 29 years later. Stated another way, from a debtor's point of view and assuming income keeps up with inflation, the payment on your 30-year mortgage will only cost half as much, relatively speaking, in that last year prior to pay-off.

Conversely, when a 30-year bond investment matures, the principal paid back to you (assuming 2.5% annual inflation) will only buy half as much. However, if the inflation rate as reported by the government during the next 30 years mirrors what it has been for the past 30 years (around 4%) then the dollar invested today will only buy 30 cents worth of goods or services in 30 years, representing a 70% erosion of your current purchasing power.

If you concluded from these examples that even modest inflation helps debtors and hurts savers, you are correct. Is this a good thing? Is this as it should be? That depends. In the time-honored struggle between the savers and borrowers, savers have typically come up on the short end of the stick. However, they also take significantly less risk.

A capitalistic society needs both savers and borrowers because the two provide the equilibrium necessary for economic growth. If savers have no one willing to borrow and make use of their savings, banks can't afford to pay any interest. If investors have no savings to borrow, then growth will be limited to what capital investors and entrepreneurs have to invest. The banks, acting as middlemen, eliminate the risk to savers, and by evaluating the risks being taken by borrowers or entrepreneurs/business owners before granting their loans, minimize the bank's risk of loss. While small business owners, entrepreneurs or venture capitalists put up the seed capital and take the majority of the risk for any investment, it is the bank, through savings deposits, that usually puts up the balance making the investment possible in the first place.

In a perfect world, savers would be compensated with a real rate of return on their money (after taxes and inflation) of a percent or two. However, as with everything else, this fluctuates with supply and demand. Remembering that we are a global economy when it comes to borrowing, if there are more savings in the world than others are willing to borrow, rates will be lower. The opposite is also true. Rates will be higher if there are more people looking to borrow than there are savings in the world to be loaned.

The world currently has a surplus of savers, mostly from Asian countries, which along with other factors, is helping to keep interest rates fairly low. This is not only good for investors who borrow money but also helps provide credit for retail purchases and tends to be good for the economy. Far fewer cars and large-ticket items would be bought if those purchases could not be made on credit and paid back over time.

This also includes credit card purchases for smaller items helping to drive the economy. Credit is the lifeblood of global growth and capitalism. As the world becomes more and more capitalistic, more and more credit is needed. This debt adds more inherent risk to the entire global economic system, especially when governments all over the world become some of the greatest debtors.

When a government is in debt and also in control of the money supply, there is an inherent conflict of interest. The temptation to simply print money to pay down debt is great and this option is too often used to the detriment of a country's currency and purchasing power. This inflation negatively impacts the lifestyles of its citizens as necessary goods and services become more and more expensive. Inflation is, in effect, a "stealth" tax—and any tax reduces what people can afford, hence, diminishing their lifestyles.

Currently, because of anemic growth that is deflationary in nature within the more developed nations, it is offsetting the otherwise inflationary tendencies that quantitative easing or printing money would typically cause. This along with deflationary forces from less developed nations exporting cheap labor via subsidized goods and services, is also offsetting the inflationary tendencies of quantitative easing. I expect this will continue for years, if not decades, as the two potential economic powerhouses, India and China, along with the other developing nations, continue to grow. As long as these countries tie their currencies somewhat to the developed world's currencies (which they must do until their economies develop enough to be self-sustaining and no longer dependent on exports), then this will give the already developed nations a good backdrop to print money without the inherent inflationary consequences.

I recall reading about a decade ago of Chinese workers being shipped on trains from the countryside where they lived to the cities where they worked—for a wage of one dollar per day. They remained in the city during the work week, returning home only on weekends but *still* lived a better lifestyle because, relatively speaking, that dollar-per-day wage was greater than what they could earn farming.

More recently, incomes in China have increased so much (again, relatively speaking) that they are beginning to lose their competitive edge to poorer countries like Vietnam and Myanmar. This is highly inflationary within China because, as Chinese incomes rise, these workers can afford to pay higher prices for goods and services. However, the relatively low levels of income in China (and the surrounding less-developed nations) remain a deflationary force from a worldwide perspective because, relative to incomes in more developed nations, these labor costs/incomes are still very low.

It is also deflationary as nations experience economic recession which many nations worldwide have experienced since the financial crisis of 2008 to 2009. Typically, inflation is held at bay somewhat during a recession. Between these deflationary forces, the central banks of the developed world have been and will continue to print their way out of the depths of their respective credit crises, and yet economically, tough times have lingered and will likely continue to do so. However, if any country via over-printing its currency creates higher inflation in an otherwise weak economy, this often leads to what is referred to as stagflation—persistent inflation combined with stagnant or negative economic growth—already being experienced in many emerging market economies.

The United States has the largest economy in the world. It is perhaps not surprising, therefore, that our government is also the largest debtor in the world. The U.S. dollar is the most widely circulated currency on the planet and has been its reserve currency for decades. What this means is that most, if not all, countries hold U.S. dollars in some form or other. U.S. currency is held mainly in debt instruments issued by the U.S. Treasury in the form of bonds, notes and treasury bills. So when we increase the monetary supply beyond our economic growth as a country, we make every dollar across the world worth a little less. You can imagine why foreign central banks sitting on trillions of our dollars in reserve grow concerned when those dollars lose value. This stealth tax affects both American citizens and the world around us because it erodes the value of every dollar out there—and of course, the U.S. debt other nations own and are holding in reserve is denominated in American dollars.

Unfortunately, too many countries in addition to the U.S. are caught in a Catch-22. They are already deficit spending which means they are spending more money than they are collecting in taxes and simply borrowing the difference, unable to raise taxes because this causes a drag on the economy. If the economy slows, they bring in even fewer dollars and have to borrow even more money just to balance the budget. If they reduce spending (social benefit payments) to try and balance the budget and create a surplus, they then risk offending their constituents who expect these social programs promised and in most cases, depend on. During the past few decades, the solution has therefore been to continue borrowing in an attempt to bridge the gap. As our debt grows, however, so do our interest payments, forcing us to borrow even more. So you can see how the government, any government in debt, has a vested interest in keeping interest rates low to service massive debt loads, keeping them as affordable as possible.

Consider this. Thinking the U.S. too far in debt, what would happen if no one would loan our government any more money? This would force the government to either raise taxes, hurting the economy, or reduce spending which ultimately deprives people of needed benefits and still hurts the economy with less government spending. Or the other option would be to print whatever amount of money is needed to bridge the gap—increasing the monetary supply and potentially causing inflation. The first two results are self-defeating because they slow the economy, bring in less revenue and create a larger gap. The latter is the only real option and is what nations have been doing for decades, ramping it up even more since the financial crisis in 2008. Developed nations and the world in general are even more in debt than in 2008—and it's that debt that is having a negative effect on global growth.

Presently, the U.S. national debt has exceeded $18 trillion. Unfortunately, the monetizing of debt (printing our way out of it) is what I believe must continue to a certain degree, and this debt will continue to get worse. But the more concerning problem here is future obligations which must also be looked at as debt. We owe it to the baby boomers who have been paying into the system for decades and are expecting promised benefits—Medicare, Social Security and government prescription drug plans—and it will cost the government approximately $50 to $70 trillion *more* based on current estimates.

This is a debt we simply cannot tax or grow our way out of unless the government adopts some extreme fundamental changes to accelerate growth. In all likelihood, we will have to inflate our way out of it, a reality that people have to consider when planning for the future. This will be a rude awakening for the baby boomers as they begin to retire en masse. The benefit payment they receive simply won't buy the amount of goods and services they anticipated and have been counting on for years.

And lest you feel this is only an American problem, think again. Japan's future obligations as well as most of Europe's (again, relatively speaking) are even greater than ours and coming on more quickly because these parts of the world have older populations than here in the U.S. Unless a number of unforeseen technologies come along to save the day, the lifestyles of retiring generations in developed nations around the world will be much lower than expected. The result will be that many potential retirees won't be able to retire and will have to work far longer than they could ever have imagined.

So what's the solution? How does a country get itself out of debt? Too often it never does, but the best way for this to take place is to *grow* its way out of debt—in the same way a household is forced to—spending less than they take in and using the difference to pay down the debt.

As the economy grows, the government collects more in taxes. If they don't increase spending at the same time, the economy continues to grow, the government will eventually take in more than it spends, and the difference or surplus would theoretically be used to pay down the debt. The hard part here is *not* increasing the spending as additional revenue flows in. This is why it is so imperative for the government and Federal Reserve to do everything in their power to keep the economy robust and growing.

In order to help this along, it is likely that the United States, the world's largest debtor, will continue to print dollars and monetize our debt to the extent that we can without causing a precipitous drop in the dollar or an unacceptable inflation rate. Currently both of these potentially negative consequences of quantitative easing (printing dollars) are well-contained. Deflationary forces worldwide are keeping inflation in check, and the dollar is actually strengthening against most currencies because of the relative strength of our economy versus other countries, particularly those of Japan and the eurozone.

Europe has done all it can, and is considering its own quantitative easing scheme to drive the euro down in an attempt to make European exports more competitive, boost their economies and create inflation. I think it is only a matter of time before the European Central Bank starts a quantitative easing program and debases the euro further in an effort to strengthen otherwise sluggish economic growth throughout Europe. Japan has had the printing presses running for years but more so in recent years as previous attempts have done little to create the economic growth and inflation needed to deal with their enormous debt levels. Theoretically, the side effect to all this quantitative easing, zero-rate policies and currency debasing would be higher inflation and interest rates.

However, I don't believe this will be the case any time soon because worldwide economic growth is too slow and higher interest rates would be a drag on what little growth is taking place. It would also tend to strengthen the currency of whatever country increased its rates, making exports less competitive. Any policies placing a drag on economic growth will be avoided as they would defeat the longer- term objective of dealing with future obligations to the retiring baby boomers and the social obligations of Japan and the European nations. Over time, this debasement of developed nations' currencies should gradually increase the value of emerging market currencies as their economies become more self-sufficient and less reliant on exports. This, however, will be years or decades in the making.

All the while, the world will continue moving toward a more and more interdependent, global economy. The Chinese will own large stakes in American companies. Indians will own large stakes in European companies. Brazilians will own large stakes in Japanese companies. Global companies from developed nations (Coca-Cola, McDonald's, BMW, BP and others) will increase business in developing nations as those countries become wealthier—and keep in mind here that about 50% of profits from Fortune 500 companies already come from foreign sources.

Eventually, as inflation sets in over the next decade, everything including wages will increase substantially except for social benefits. They will increase but only slightly, forcing people in developed nations to work longer in order to supplement their own relatively meager Social Security benefits. By working longer they will also continue contributing to needed tax revenues. This will be necessary to prevent overtaxing the younger generations. Lifestyles will then stagnate in developed nations as the lifestyles of people around the world become more homogenized. This will occur as all societies become more sophisticated and global in nature while technology continues to make this world a far more interconnected, smaller place.

I expect that, toward the end of this decade or early in the next, technological advancements will begin reducing the relative cost of healthcare and energy, moderating today's big budget busters worldwide and ushering in a new global prosperity which will be reflected in global assets, global markets and enhanced lifestyles worldwide.

I also suspect the world will become a more peaceful place again, relatively speaking, as all nations become more economically vested in one another with far more to lose from waging war than they could ever hope to gain. This is the beauty and the benefit of capitalism in what I predict will be ever-expanding free societies, worldwide.

ABOUT THE AUTHOR

Douglas Obey has been serving people as a financial advisor for more than 30 years. When he became certified as a financial planner in 1987 there were fewer than 1000 CFPs nationwide; now there are more than 6,000 registered in his home state of Massachusetts alone.

Douglas is a self-made, successful entrepreneur and business owner who has acted as CFO and advisor to many other business owners. Although he earned a degree in architectural engineering, once he whet his appetite in the financial industry, his fascination and vision turned straight to economics. This passion grew into a multi-faceted study of economics ultimately backed by many years of solid experience.

Obey's premise, developed by years of experience, is that self-interest is the motivation behind everything we do—that self-interest dictates family dynamics, societal norms and collectively, our world as a whole. It is the driving force behind our human condition.